T175 NETWORKED LIVIN

Exploring Information an
Communication Technologies

Block 3
Entertainment and information
Parts 1–2

Prepared on behalf of the course team
by Chris Bissell and David Chapman

This publication forms part of an Open University course T175 *Networked living*. Details of this and other Open University courses can be obtained from the Student Registration and Enquiry Service, The Open University, PO Box 197, Milton Keynes MK7 6BJ, United Kingdom: tel. +44 (0)870 333 4340, email general-enquiries@open.ac.uk

Alternatively, you may visit the Open University website at http://www.open.ac.uk where you can learn more about the wide range of courses and packs offered at all levels by The Open University.

To purchase a selection of Open University course materials visit http://www.ouw.co.uk, or contact Open University Worldwide, Michael Young Building, Walton Hall, Milton Keynes MK7 6AA, United Kingdom for a brochure. tel. +44 (0)1908 858785; fax +44 (0)1908 858787; e-mail ouwenq@open.ac.uk

The Open University
Walton Hall, Milton Keynes
MK7 6AA

First published 2005. Second edition 2006.

Edited and designed by The Open University.

Typeset in India by Alden Prepress Services, Chennai

Printed and bound in the United Kingdom by Halstan Printing Group, Amersham.

ISBN 978 0 7492 1521 7

2.1

The paper used in this publication contains pulp sourced from forests independently certified to the Forest Stewardship Council (FSC) principles and criteria. Chain of custody certification allows the pulp from these forests to be tracked to the end use (see www.fsc-uk.org).

Course Team List

Karen Kear, course team chair

Ernie Taylor, course manager

Patricia Telford, course secretary

Academic staff

Mustafa Ali

Chris Bissell

David Chapman

Geoff Einon

Clem Herman

Allan Jones

Roger Jones

John Monk

Nicky Moss

Elaine Thomas

Mirabelle Walker

Judith Williams

John Woodthorpe

Media production staff

Geoff Austin

Deirdre Bethune

Annette Booz

Sophia Braybrooke

Sarah Crompton

Jamie Daniels

Vicky Eves

Alison George

Mark Kesby

Lynn Short

External assessor

Professor Philip Witting, University of Glamorgan

Contents

Part 1
Entertainment

Chris Bissell

1 Introduction

This block will be concerned with both the technological aspects of ICTs, and some of the ways they are used and regulated in contemporary society. The context of the Block is 'entertainment and information', two major application areas of ICTs. You'll be asked to apply quite a few of the things you learnt earlier in the course to these new applications.

Figure 1 is a repeat of a generic diagram of a communication system introduced earlier in the course. But it can also be applied to many of the ways ICTs are used for entertainment and in collecting information.

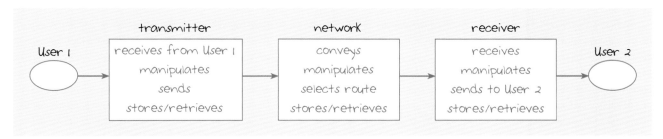

Figure 1 A generic communication system

For example, in digital broadcasting, User 1 might be the production company that generates and records an audio or TV programme. The transmitter would be owned by a broadcasting or other company, and would take the file prepared by User 1, manipulate it into a form suitable for broadcasting, and transmit it by terrestrial, satellite or cable means. Precisely what functions the network carries out would depend on which of these means is used. For terrestrial digital broadcasting, there might be route selection in order to send the data to a number of different transmitters. For satellite or cable distribution, again there would probably be a need to select routes at some point in the system, possibly with intermediate storage. At the receiver, the file is manipulated into a form suitable to be seen or heard by User 2, the viewer or listener. For a broadcast service there would be many such users, so the diagram should really be modified to reflect this, by adding additional receiver and user blocks at the right-hand side.

Activity 1 (exploratory)

Figure 2 is based on the diagram used earlier in the course to represent a stand-alone computer. If used as shown to represent a stand-alone DVD player, suggest some functions carried out by the DVD player in each category.

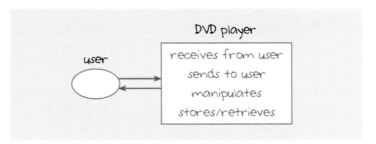

Figure 2 Representation of a DVD player

Comment

Your answer to this will depend on your experience with DVD players, and the type of equipment in common use when you read this. However, you may have suggested some of the following:

- receives information from the user about play, pause, fast forward, select subtitles, etc.; may store such information in internal memory
- retrieves the data from disk
- manipulates the data read from disk into the appropriate audio and video signals
- sends to user the audio and video signals via integral or separate TV or hi-fi system.

1.1 Time, space and ICTs

Before we turn to technological aspects of entertainment products and services, I would like you to think about the wider context of ICTs in a range of applications.

Activity 2 (exploratory)

Think about the benefits often claimed for ICTs – for example, in the media, by governments, and by manufacturers and providers of services. What key words or phrases come to mind? (Hint: Think about advertisements for entertainment and communication products; and government or local council 'consultation documents', if you've seen any. What does your local school or library say about ICTs?)

Comment

What you answer here will depend on when you read this, and on your background in ICT. I am writing this in mid-2005. I am inundated with advertisements for broadband internet access; digital TV options; mobile phones with video; laptop and palmtop computers; and so on.

Libraries now emphasise computer workstations, the internet, CDs and DVDs almost as much as books. The sorts of keywords, phrases, and images used in advertising and other documents are:

- choice, fast, available, accessible
- freedom of movement (mobile phones, PDAs, DVD players, etc.)
- instant communication anywhere, anytime
- immediate satisfaction
- crystal-clear sound and images
- improved democracy
- access to information and services
- information revolution
- e-learning and e-government.

One of the features sometimes stressed about ICTs is the way they can 'reorganise time and space' for both entertainment and information. You have already met one aspect of this – the time aspect – in the distinction made earlier between synchronous and asynchronous communication.

The idea of ICTs having the potential to reorganise time and space has a long history. For example, the printed book – an early example of an information and communication technology – provided an easily portable, standardised form of communication. Economies of scale meant that the price of popular printed books (such as the Bible) could be kept comparatively low. Different people, at different times, in different places, could read an identical text – something very different from the days when communication and dissemination of information meant messengers travelling from place to place to read out proclamations.

Activity 3 (exploratory)

Think about the following examples of ICT systems in the context of entertainment. What are their availability in time and space? Think about the potential location of the user, and any restrictions on times of access to the information. Either fill in your thoughts in a grid like Table 1, or make a list.

Table 1

System	Availability in time	Availability in space
Radio and TV broadcasting		
Film (cinema)		
Video / DVD		
The internet		

Comment

- Portable radio and television receivers mean that traditional broadcasting is independent of the location of the recipient (within geographical limits) but restricted in time. Without integral or separate audio or video recording you have to tune in at the time a programme is broadcast.

- In principle, film is independent of both time and space (if you've got the right equipment, you can show a film anywhere, at any time). But for most people, you have to visit a particular cinema at a certain time.

- Video/DVD is independent of both time and space to a greater extent, at least within large towns with a good range of video shops or libraries. Home off-air recording eliminates the time restrictions of conventional broadcasting. However, different standards may exist in different countries or geographical areas.

- The internet can be independent of both time and space (providing there is network access). This is one reason why broadcasters are increasingly making programmes and programme archives available via the Web.

It's worth noting that as technology evolves, the distinctions identified in this activity are changing. For example, television broadcasting is increasingly becoming integrated with DVD or hard-disk storage, allowing users much more flexibility in when they watch programmes.

1.2 Utopias

Another feature of ICTs is the way they are often presented in a highly positive way as an answer to human problems. ICTs – as we are repeatedly told – will revolutionise our personal lives, bring untold commercial and social benefits, and transform society and education. There is nothing new in this **utopian** vision of technology.

utopian

The word utopia was coined in 1516 as the title of a book by Sir Thomas More. His *Utopia* was an imaginary island representing the perfect society.

Activity 4 (exploratory)

Read the following extracts concerning a number of technologies developed over the last 200 years. I have deleted references to the particular technologies, indicated by ***.

What do you think the extracts refer to, and when do you think the claim was made? You'll recall that the symbol '...' (an ellipsis), indicates that some parts of the quotation that are irrelevant to the current discussion have been omitted. Square brackets are used to indicate any change to a quotation. (I'll say more about this convention later.)

1   The *** allowed people to communicate almost instantly across great distances, in effect shrinking the world faster and further than ever before. *** revolutionised business practice, gave rise to new forms of crime and inundated its users with a deluge of information. Romances blossomed. [...] Secret codes were devised by some users, and cracked by others. Governments and regulators tried and failed to control the new medium. Attitudes to everything from newsgathering to diplomacy had to be completely rethought. Meanwhile, [...] a technological subculture with its own customs and vocabulary was establishing itself.

2   *** is destined to revolutionise our educational system and in a few years it will supplant largely, if not entirely, the use of textbooks.

3   *** are capable of transforming society. Far from being over, the *** revolution that created the *** has barely begun. These technologies will change almost every aspect of our lives – private, social, cultural, economic and political.

4   ***: its probable destination as a channel of intelligence: general ideas of its power as an agent of communication. The ***: its wonderful properties; annihilates time; unaffected by position.

Comment

1   Telegraph. (Standage, Tom (1999) *The Victorian Internet, The Remarkable Story of the Telegraph and the Nineteenth Century's Online Pioneers*, London: Phoenix)

2   Film (motion pictures). (Attributed to Thomas Edison, 1922)

3   ICTs; information; internet. (*Economist*, 25 January 2003)

4   Electricity; telegraph. (*The Silent Revolution. Or, The Future Effects of Steam and Electricity upon the Condition of Mankind*, by Michael Angelo Garvey, 1852)

The point about this activity is to ask you to think critically about information and communication technologies and systems. Did the answers surprise you, or not? It is easy to make exaggerated claims about the power of technologies, not only when they are new or revolutionary, but also in retrospect. I'm not denying that all the technologies and systems of the previous activity have brought about huge changes in our lives. But films have certainly not replaced textbooks, and the utopian predictions often made in the past about electricity and the telegraph, for example, have fallen well short of the mark. Many similar predictions are currently being made about the internet which may also turn out to be inaccurate!

Similar utopian claims have been made in the past about canals, railways and automobiles as forces for liberation, improved communication and human harmony. I'll not discuss the accuracy or otherwise of such claims any further here, but it is useful to make one further point about

all these technologies: they came into their own only with the creation of an appropriate corresponding large-scale system (including a system for manufacturing the necessary system components) – and, in particular, a network. The first canal, or railway, was of limited use without the subsequent large-scale connectivity that brought about improved communication. In this respect these transport systems certainly show similarities with the development of ICTs.

2 Digital ICTs

In this part of Block 3 I'll be introducing the idea that most ICT systems are now digital, explaining what that means, and discussing why this should be so. The context will be the entertainment industries, where ICTs are exploited on a huge scale. I'll present just a few aspects of such technologies, and also some important issues arising from the digitisation of entertainment products. Most examples will be taken from the representation of images: stills as in digital photography, for example; digital video as in DVDs and digital TV; or animations as in computer games.

Activity 5 (exploratory)

Identify some examples where digital technologies are used in entertainment activities or products. (Even if you don't know much about the technologies, think of a few buzzwords containing the term 'digital' or relating to these new technologies.)

Comment

I thought of:

- digital radio and TV broadcasting
- digital production and recording of music and video
- digital control of lighting etc. for concerts and clubs
- computer games
- digital special effects and even 'digital actors' in cinema
- digital cameras (still and video).

There are many other examples.

2.1 Thinking digital

Information and communication technologies often rely on representing some aspect of the real world in a form that can be stored, transmitted or manipulated. There are two major ways of doing this. The first has come to be known as **analogue** representation. In analogue representations, the representation is a direct counterpart (analogue) of the real-world aspect that we are trying to capture. Let me try to make this concept clearer using the example of audible sound.

analogue

What we call 'sound' is rapid variations (up to about 20 000 per second) in pressure, transmitted through the air or some other medium such as water or metal. Apart from when underwater swimming, we're normally concerned with pressure variations transmitted through the air that cause the ear drum to vibrate, and a neural signal to be transmitted to the brain.

In analogue sound recording, the variations in air pressure were converted to a corresponding variation in electrical voltage or current (using a microphone), and then into a corresponding variation in a wavy groove in a vinyl record, or magnetisation of a cassette tape (Figure 3). Until the end of the twentieth century many of the technologies used to store or transmit information were analogue in form: telephony, radio, television, vinyl discs and magnetic tape recording, for example.

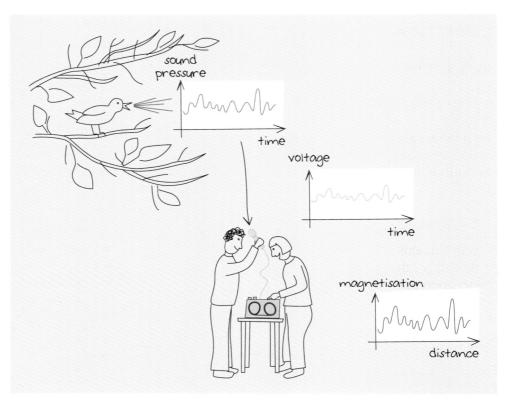

Figure 3   Analogue recording

An important feature of almost all analogue signals of interest to us is that they vary continuously over a given range. For example, within audible limits, the intensity of a sound can take on any value; similarly, the analogue voltage or current used to represent it can take on any value in a corresponding range.

digital

The second type of representation is known as **digital**. In digital representations, codes using a limited set of symbols are used to represent the original information. Morse code is an example of a digital coding scheme. Three symbols (dot, dash and space) are used to code any message (Figure 4).

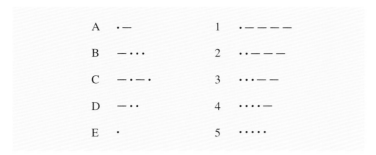

Figure 4 Part of the Morse code

One key factor in the rise of digital ICTs is that any analogue signal can, in principle, be converted into a corresponding digital one, by using codes to represent the original analogue signal. For example, consider measuring temperature. Temperature, by its nature, can take on any value within a given range, and is thus **continuous**. So when temperature is measured by a traditional mercury- or alcohol-in-glass thermometer, we have a continuous, analogue representation (the level of the liquid column in the glass tube). Just as the temperature itself can take on any value in a given range, so can the level of the liquid in the thermometer.

continuous

But a common alternative way of measuring and displaying temperature is to use a sensor to convert the temperature into an electrical voltage. At this stage, the representation is an analogue voltage – but to display the temperature it is normal to use an electronic circuit to convert the analogue voltage into a digital representation, as a numerical value of degrees centigrade or Fahrenheit. For a room thermometer, such a display would probably be to the nearest degree. In this case, a temperature of, say, 25.8 degrees would appear as 26 degrees. Even a more accurate digital thermometer designed for scientific or medical purposes, for example, can use only a finite number of digits in a display.

Activity 6 (self-assessment)

What are the essential differences between 'analogue' and 'digital' representations?

Comment

My answer is given at the end of this part.

2.2 Digital images

In principle, digital codes can be used to represent any type of information. Since this part of Block 3 takes entertainment as its theme, let's start with images on a computer (or mobile phone) screen, an increasingly important aspect of entertainment in the 'digital world'.

pixels

On a computer screen, images are generated by dividing the display into a large number of tiny units called **pixels** (from 'picture elements'). Each pixel can in general be displayed in a number of different colours and brightnesses. The greater the number of pixels used for a given size of display, and the greater the number of colours, then the higher the quality of the image. To begin with, we'll look at the representation of black and white images, and come back to colours later.

Let's consider an artificially small-scale example, a display using eight rows of sixteen pixels. In Figure 5, I have shown how this system could display a triangular outline.

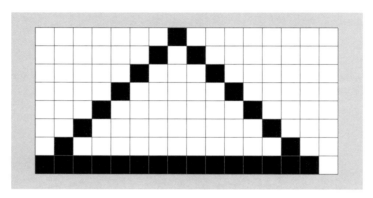

Figure 5 Black on white triangular outline on an eight by sixteen pixel display

Activity 7 (exploratory)

What do you notice about the representation of the three sides of the 'triangle'?

Comment

The horizontal side is a perfect straight line, since all the pixels are lined up along the row. The other sides have a 'staircase' appearance, and only approximate a straight line. You may well have noticed this effect on mobile phone displays or computer games.

This 'staircase' effect is an important feature of digital displays. Figure 6 shows an example using the Windows Paint program (one of the programs in Accessories) to draw a simple geometrical shape, using a thick line width. Next time you use your computer, draw some simple shapes with Paint, and 'zoom in' (an option under the View menu) to examine this effect in detail.

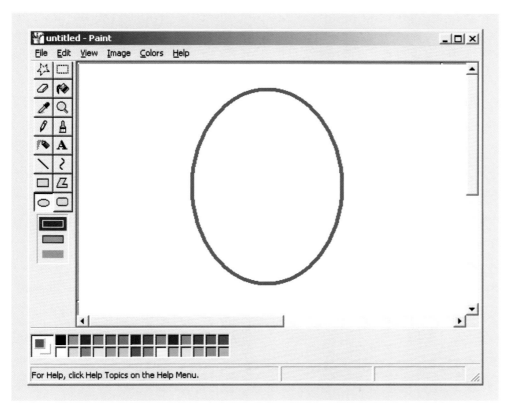

Figure 6 A shape drawn with the Windows Paint program

I noted above that a defining feature of digital techniques is the representation of the information by codes. Let's look now at how that can be done for the simple triangular image of Figure 5.

Information is stored, processed and transmitted digitally in a great variety of ways. One of the most common is **binary** representation. In binary representation just two symbols or 'states' are used. Inside a computer these binary states could be two different values of an electrical voltage or electrical charge. In magnetic storage media, such as a hard disk or magnetic tape, two different patterns of magnetisation are used. For transmission over optical fibres, the two states are the presence or absence of a short pulse of laser light. In CDs and DVDs the two states are differently shaped microscopic indentations in the surface of the disk, which can be detected by shining laser light onto the disc.

binary

The two states of binary are represented in writing as 0 and 1. So, for example, a low electrical voltage could represent a binary 0, and a higher voltage a binary 1. Or the 0 could be represented by an absence of a pulse of laser light, and the 1 by a pulse of such light. For most of this course we'll not be concerned with precisely what physical quantities are used for the binary 1s and 0s, but we shall be concerned with how to use binary coding for the transmission and processing of information.

Let's get back to our image of a triangle. If we represent a white pixel by a binary 0, and a black pixel by a 1, we can code the image as follows:

0 0 0 0 0 0 0 1 0 0 0 0 0 0 0 0

0 0 0 0 0 0 1 0 1 0 0 0 0 0 0 0

0 0 0 0 0 1 0 0 0 1 0 0 0 0 0 0

0 0 0 0 1 0 0 0 0 0 1 0 0 0 0 0

0 0 0 1 0 0 0 0 0 0 0 1 0 0 0 0

0 0 1 0 0 0 0 0 0 0 0 0 1 0 0 0

0 1 0 0 0 0 0 0 0 0 0 0 0 1 0 0

1 1 1 1 1 1 1 1 1 1 1 1 1 1 1 0

We've now converted the image into a set of binary ones and zeros that we could store or transmit using any digital technique at our disposal. Provided we always use the same conventions (for example: 0 = white; 1 = black; display of 16×8 pixels read from top left to bottom right) we can reconstruct the image pixel by pixel.

Activity 8 (self-assessment)

Figure 5 is a black triangle on a white background. How would you code a similar white triangle on a black background using this simple scheme?

Comment

The answer is given at the end of this part.

This is a very simple illustration of the enormous potential of digital processing. Once we have coded the information in digital form, all sorts of possibilities for manipulating the information arise. For example, by means of a simple instruction we can make overall changes to an image, such as changing black to white – or one colour into another, as you will see later. This technique lies at the heart of many more complex processing functions – not only for images, but also for text and sound, as you will see later in this block.

The display system described so far is simple, but restricted. By increasing the number of pixels we can improve the resolution, so as to get high-quality black and white images.

The screen of the computer I am using to write this allows a range of display options between 800×600 pixels and 1600×1200, but screens using larger numbers of pixels are rapidly becoming available, and may well be standard by the time you study this. Increasing the resolution means that increasing numbers of pixels must be coded and stored. To get an idea of the numbers of pixels involved in a practical situation, try the following two activities.

Activity 9 (self-assessment)

(a) What is the total number of pixels in the display for the lower and higher resolutions just mentioned?

(b) What is the ratio of the two totals (the higher divided by the lower)?

You could use the Windows calculator to work these out.

4

800 × 600 = 480 000
1600 × 1200 = 1920 000

Comment

The answer is given at the end of this part.

Activity 10 (exploratory)

The answer to question (b) of Activity 9 was 4. Can you explain this value in terms of the numbers of pixels vertically and horizontally in the two options?

Comment

The higher resolution uses double the number of pixels both horizontally and vertically, so the total number over the whole of the screen area is $2 \times 2 = 4$ times as great. In fact, this is an important general rule: double the number of pixels horizontally and vertically and you quadruple the total number.

But what about improving the representation by including shades of grey or different colours?

Suppose we want to code a rather more colourful version of our original triangle such as the one in Figure 7. We have four colours now: red, blue, black and white.

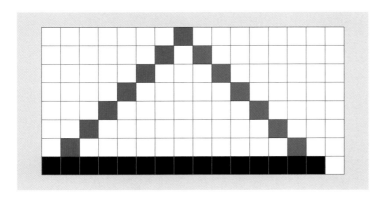

Figure 7   A triangle with four colours

We can extend our binary representation of each pixel as follows. Instead of just one binary digit (a zero or one), we can use two for each pixel. A binary digit is usually known as a bit; a bit can take only the value 0 or 1. But by allocating two bits to each colour, we can still code the pixels digitally as we now have four possible codes. For example:

```
00 white

01 red

10 blue

11 black
```

So the binary, digital coding of the coloured triangle would be, with two bits per pixel:

```
00 00 00 00 00 00 00 01 00 00 00 00 00 00 00 00

00 00 00 00 00 00 01 00 10 00 00 00 00 00 00 00

00 00 00 00 00 01 00 00 00 10 00 00 00 00 00 00

00 00 00 00 01 00 00 00 00 00 10 00 00 00 00 00

00 00 00 01 00 00 00 00 00 00 00 10 00 00 00 00

00 00 01 00 00 00 00 00 00 00 00 00 10 00 00 00

00 01 00 00 00 00 00 00 00 00 00 00 00 10 00 00

11 11 11 11 11 11 11 11 11 11 11 11 11 11 11 00
```

Activity 11 (self-assessment)

Suppose that all the zeros in the above coded image are changed to ones, and all the ones converted to zeros. Describe the resulting image.

Comment

The answer is given at the end of this part.

Binary coding can be extended to represent an increasing range of colours. For eight colours, for example, we need to use three bits for each. The actual allocation of colours to codes is arbitrary, but there has to be an agreed standard to ensure **interoperability** – in other words, so that software produced by different companies will result in the same colours being displayed on computers from different manufacturers. (I'll have a lot more to say about standards in later sections.)

interoperability

The following scheme is used in practice for those situations where each colour is represented by three bits:

    000 black

    001 red

    010 green

    011 yellow

    100 blue

    101 magenta

    110 cyan

    111 white

(In colour optics terminology, magenta is a mixture of red and blue light; cyan is a mixture of blue and green.)

Perhaps you can see the general pattern in the construction of the new 3-bit codes used for the colours. To get the eight codes, we take the four codes of the previous system:

    00

    01

    10

    11

Then we put a binary 0 in front of each, to generate four new, 3-bit, codes:

    000

    001

    010

    011

Next we put a binary 1 in front of the four original codes to generate another four new codes:

    100

    101

    110

    111

A set of a given number of bits used for data representation (in general, not just for colours) is called a **binary word**: in this example we have eight, 3-bit, binary words to represent the eight different colours.

binary word

Activity 12 (self-assessment)

How long must a binary word be to represent 16 different colours? Write out the 16 code words.

Comment

My answer is given at the end of this part.

Any coding scheme that allocates a binary code to each pixel in order to define its colour and brightness is called a **bitmap**. The term is usually restricted to coding schemes that code these values directly – normally to computer files with the extension .bmp that can be displayed by a wide range of software.

Other techniques that I'll be introducing later (such as JPEG) use information about human perception to reduce file sizes. They still assign binary codes to pixels, but in a different way, and are not usually called 'bitmaps'.

It's also worth mentioning here a very different approach to coding images, known as **vector graphics**. In a vector graphic representation, instead of sending or storing information about each pixel, information about the different shapes in the image is used. Vector graphics are most appropriate where the image is made up of regular shapes, as is the case in many Web or computer game graphics. For example, a straight line can be defined simply by its starting and end points, or a circle by its centre and radius. In this way, file sizes can be kept much smaller than a bitmap, provided the complete graphic consists only of the shapes allowed within the vector graphic system. It is also easy to produce simple animations of such shapes. For images such as photographs or motion pictures, however, the vector graphics approach is not effective.

bitmap
You will come across the term bitmap used in two ways: (a) to describe a particular approach to image coding; (b) to describe the actual images generated by such coding.

vector graphics

2.3 The binary numbers game

In your study of ICTs you will need to be familiar with the way binary representations work. I've chosen to discuss the representation of images, but the same general principles apply to the representation of sounds, texts, and other sources of information.

So far you have seen that a 1-bit binary word can represent two colour options; a 2-bit word can represent four; a 3-bit word can represent eight; and a 4-bit word sixteen.

Can you see the pattern here? Each time you increase the length of the word by one bit, you double the number of different binary codes possible, as listed in Table 2.

Table 2 Relationship between number of bits in a word and number of binary codes

Word length (bits)	Number of codes
1	2
2	4
3	8
4	16
5	32
6	64
7	128
8	256
9	512
10	1024
11	2048
12	4096

We can also show this in graph form. I've shown this as a spreadsheet chart for 1- to 10-bit words in Figure 8. You'll produce a chart like this as part of the computer activities associated with this block.

Note how rapidly the number of codes increases as the word length increases. This sort of growth has a particularly important characteristic: one quantity (in this case, the number of codes) increases by a given *factor* (in this case, multiplying by a factor of two) every time another quantity (in this case, the word length) is increased by a given *amount* (in this case adding one extra bit). This sort of growth is called **exponential growth**. You will come across a number of examples of exponential growth in this block.

exponential growth

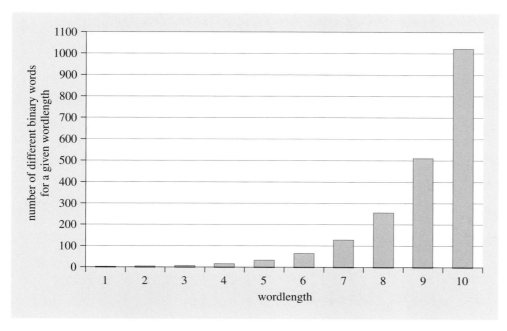

Figure 8 Chart view of Table 2

Activity 13 (exploratory)

In a savings account, the amount invested gains interest at a constant percentage rate per year. If the interest rate is a constant 5% per annum, for example, and I do not make any further investments or withdrawals, the amount in my account at the end of the year will be 1.05 times what it was at the beginning.

Assume that the interest rate stays constant, that I make no further investments, and that I leave the money (including the interest) in the account for several years. Is this an example of exponential growth?

Comment

Yes, it is exponential growth. The initial investment increases by a given factor, determined by the interest rate, for each increase in the amount of time. In my examples the amount increases by a factor of 1.05 every year.

exponent

The term 'exponential' comes from the mathematical term **exponent**. Exponent or 'exponential' notation gives us an alternative way of expressing the numbers in the second column of Table 2. Look at Column 2 in Table 3.

Table 3

Word length (bits)	Number of codes
1	2
2	$4 = 2 \times 2$
3	$8 = 2 \times 2 \times 2$
4	$16 = 2 \times 2 \times 2 \times 2$
5	$32 = 2 \times 2 \times 2 \times 2 \times 2$
6	$64 = 2 \times 2 \times 2 \times 2 \times 2 \times 2$

You're probably already familiar with the notation 2^2 ('two squared') = $2 \times 2 = 4$. Similarly we can write:

2^3 ('two cubed') = $2 \times 2 \times 2 = 8$

2^4 ('two to the fourth') = $2 \times 2 \times 2 \times 2 = 16$

2^5 ('two to the fifth') = $2 \times 2 \times 2 \times 2 \times 2 = 32$

2^6 ('two to the sixth') = $2 \times 2 \times 2 \times 2 \times 2 \times 2 = 64$

In this notation the small number written to the top right is the 'exponent' or 'power'. It represents the number of times the other number (in normal font) is multiplied together.

There is a general way of indicating this pattern, using the symbol n to stand for the number of 2s multiplied together. Then we can write that an n-bit binary word can represent 2^n different options (say 'two to

the *n*'). Here the letter '*n*' is used to represent an arbitrary whole number; this is a common convention in science and technology.

Activity 14 (self-assessment)

Suppose we want to use a binary code to represent each of 300 colours. Look back at Table 2 and see if you can say how long each codeword would need to be.

Comment

The answer is given at the end of this part.

Now that you've seen some of the basics of binary representations of images, let's have a look at some real-world implications. Consider, for example, the following general questions (I don't want you to try to answer them now; I'll ask you to do some calculations of actual values shortly):

- How large is the data file for a single image, for an image of suitable quality?

- How long would it take a user to download such images from the internet?

- Is it possible to use this sort of digital representation of images to provide moving pictures (about 25 images per second are required for a video not to appear jerky)?

Activity 15 (self-assessment)

A common bitmap format for displaying reasonably high-quality computer images, such as those generated by digital cameras, is to use 24 bits for each pixel.

(a) How many pixels are required for 1024×768 screen resolution? How many bits of data does this require for each image?

(b) At the time of writing this, I am still using a '56 kbps' dial-up modem that connects (if I'm lucky) at 44 kbps. Roughly how long would such an image take to download at 44 kbps?

(c) By the time you read this my broadband connection will be installed, operating at 512 kbps, if not more. How long will a single image take to download over a 512 kbps connection?

(d) My DVD drive sends data to a computer processor at about 3 Mbps. Roughly how long would it take to transfer one image? Try to answer this question without using a calculator, by comparing the DVD transfer rate with the broadband rate.

Comment

The answer is given at the end of this part.

This activity has given us some rough answers to my first two bullet points above. So the answer to the third is that there is no way any of these systems could provide the 25 images per second needed for real-time video. Later in this block we'll look at how such limitations can be overcome, so that we can have video clips or even whole movies distributed at comparatively modest data rates over the internet or other network.

You will find associated computer (spreadsheet) activities in Part 3, Sections 3.1 and 3.2. You may choose to do these now, or leave it until it is more convenient. Depending on your familiarity with spreadsheets, you may need to study Part 3, Section 2, first.

2.4   Why go digital?

The previous section has indicated how images can be coded digitally. But what are the advantages of digital technologies for ICTs?

One advantage has already been mentioned: the ease with which digital data can be processed. I gave examples of changing the colours of a simple image, just by changing all binary 0s into 1s and vice versa. Once an image (or indeed any other source of information) is coded in digital form, the power of digital computers can be harnessed for easy editing, generation of special effects, copying, and so on.

Dealing with errors

A second important feature of digital coding is the way errors can be detected and even corrected. Suppose an original file (audio, video, still image, etc.) is coded in binary form, and transmitted as a stream of bits over a communications channel. No matter what is used to represent the binary zeros and ones (laser light or electrical voltages, for example), there is always some chance that a bit will be misinterpreted. If electrical voltages are used, for example, interference from other electrical machinery or devices can result in a 0 being misinterpreted as a 1 or vice versa.

There are various techniques that can be used to combat noise and interference, but those that can be used with digitally encoded signals are particularly powerful. Suppose that there is a small chance that a binary symbol will be misinterpreted. Then one simple way of reducing the error rate is to transmit each bit three times. So the sequence

1 1 0 1 0 1 1 0 0

would be transmitted

    111 111 000 111 000 111 111 000 000

Now, if a single error occurs in any triplet, it is still possible to infer what the correct sequence should have been, by adopting a 'best of three' decoding strategy within each triplet.

Suppose that when the sequence

    111 111 000 111 000 111 111 000 000

is transmitted, the sequence

    111 101 000 111 100 111 111 001 010

is received, with a total of four errors, one in each of the second, fifth, eighth and ninth triplets.

These triplets will still be interpreted as the original

    1 1 0 1 0 1 1 0 0

since no triplet contains more than one error, and the 'best of three' strategy has been successful.

Only if more than one bit in any triplet is in error will the sequence be decoded incorrectly. In this example there were four errors in 27 bits, and at this error rate it would be very likely that fairly soon there would be two separate errors in one triplet. But in practical systems, the likelihood of any single error is very much lower, and such a 'transmit three times' scheme can be extremely reliable.

Activity 16 (exploratory)

Such an improvement in performance comes at a cost. Can you suggest what this is?

Comment

The 'best of three' strategy has increased the number of bits used to code the information by a factor of three. So either the file will take three times longer to send, or the bit rate will have to be increased by a factor of three. This means that it will be more expensive (in time or money or both) to store or transmit the information. And there is an extra 'overhead' in the additional processing needed to construct the 'triplet' format, and then to check it for errors on decoding.

It is also worth mentioning that transmitting a bitstream at a higher rate can result in a greater proportion of errors. The precise design of error correction systems therefore requires careful consideration of a number of such 'trade-offs'.

redundancy

Transmitting a greater number of bits than is strictly necessary to code the original information is known as 'adding **redundancy**'. If there is no possibility of error, then two out of the three bits in each triplet are redundant. Adding redundancy, however, gives us the means to combat errors. In the triplet example we could say that there is 2/3 = 67% redundancy.

Activity 17 (self-assessment)

Suppose, instead of transmitting each bit three times, each was transmitted only twice. If there is a single error in the received data, could it be detected? Could it be corrected? Compare the amount of redundancy in the transmitted data with that in the triplet example.

Comment

The answer is given at the end of this part.

error detecting code

error correcting code

Transmitting each bit twice is an example of an **error detecting code**, whereas the triplet scheme is an **error correcting code**. Error detecting codes can be used when, for example, a receiver can request the retransmission of data known to contain an error (in some internet applications, for example). If there is no possibility of requesting a repeat, error correcting codes are often used (in transmitting images from deep space, for example, when the signal may take hours or even days to reach Earth).

Now, there are many, far more powerful, error detection and correction techniques used in modern ICT systems than the simple ones just described. But all of them carry some sort of cost in increasing the total amount of data to be transmitted or processed, and in adding processing overheads. The type of error protection that is appropriate depends on the nature of the information being transmitted. In many cases, the occasional bit in error will not detract from the value of the information (a telephone conversation, for example). In other cases (a computer program, for example), even one bit in error might render the information completely useless.

To recap, by incorporating enough redundancy, in an appropriate manner, we can make the transmission of information in digital form highly reliable, giving potentially much higher-quality sound and images in entertainment and other products than was possible in earlier, analogue systems.

A common technology

There is a third important advantage of 'going digital', and one that has had a huge effect on making viable the development of high-tech digital devices and systems. It is that a common digital technology can be used for a variety of sources of information. Until recently text, audio, video,

film were all completely separate in the technologies they used. For example, the sound recording system developed for film (motion pictures) in the early part of the twentieth century used an optically recorded soundtrack placed alongside the movie images. In this technique, illustrated in Figure 9, the sound wave of the soundtrack is converted into a continuously varying optical pattern printed alongside the images. A light is shone through the optical track, and a sensor converts the varying light intensity to an electrical signal which then feeds an amplifier and speakers.

Figure 9   Frames from a 1960s film with optical soundtrack (source: Ronald Grant Archive)

Activity 18 (self-assessment)

Is the optical soundtrack of such a film an analogue or digital representation?

Comment

The answer is given at the end of this part.

The sound system of the cinema was completely different in character from other audio recording systems such as vinyl disc or magnetic tape. The rise of ICT, however, has gone hand in hand with an increasing commonality in digital techniques. For example, the coding schemes developed for movies, digital photography and MP3 music files have a great deal in common. This means that all such files can be processed and recorded in a similar way – basically by means of computer hardware and software – something that brings about significant commercial advantages. I'll return to this point in a later section.

Yet another factor in the rise of digital techniques was the enormous expansion of the internet in the 1990s, particularly since the development of the Web. As a universal digital network became available to an increasing number of people, the advantages of storing, processing and transmitting information in digital form became ever more clear.

Activity 19 (self-assessment)

In the above discussion I identified three advantages of digital technologies for ICTs. What are they? Give an example for each.

Comment

My answer is given at the end of this part.

Digital recording, processing and transmission, then, offer great advantages. But there are problems, particularly with the huge amounts of data generated in, for example, moving pictures: problems for both storage and transmission, which will be considered later.

2.5   Revolution or evolution?

The aims of this block include introducing you to social aspects of ICTs, as well as the purely technical ones. In this section I want to consider some general issues relating to the ways in which new technologies are developed, introduced, and succeed or fail.

It is easy, in retrospect, to view technological developments as somehow inevitable. For instance, it seems to go without saying that we have electric refrigerators, rather than gas ones. Yet for a few years in the early part of the twentieth century there was great competition between gas and electric fridges, and it wasn't obvious that one type was going to win.

substitution technology

One useful distinction to make in technological change is between substitution technologies and supplementary technologies. A **substitution technology** is one that completely replaces another – the

way the internal combustion engine rapidly replaced other early automobile designs such as those using steam power.

A **supplementary technology** is one that continues to coexist alongside an earlier technology for a considerable time. An example is the way analogue magnetic tape recordings in the form of audiocassettes continued alongside vinyl records for many years. Both have now been substantially replaced by the digital techniques such as in CD, DVD or MP3 players, etc., at least for most commercial recordings.

supplementary technology

Activity 20 (exploratory)

Can you think of other examples of substitution and supplementary technologies in the ICT field, particularly for information and entertainment purposes?

Comment

I thought of the following examples (again in 2005):

- Fax continues to exist alongside the supplementary technology of email (although computer-generated faxes quickly took off in the 1990s and are widely used).

- DVD appears to be substituting videotape cassettes, at least for pre-recorded movies – and writable DVDs or hard-disk video recorders are rapidly increasing their market share for home off-air recording, for example.

- Video-on-demand narrowcasting has not substituted the video shop/library/postal service (narrowcasting means the targeting of a programme to individual listeners or viewers, rather than broadcasting it to everyone within a certain area).

- The telephone did not replace the telegraph and, later, telex (a commercial system similar to the telegraph) until the end of the twentieth century.

- Digital radio and TV broadcasting continues alongside analogue broadcasting (replacement will be due as much to political decisions as technological characteristics).

- Television and home video have not replaced cinema.

- Mobile telephony has not yet replaced land lines (in the UK and many industrialised countries most people have both).

These examples also illustrate the complexity of this issue. Factors that are important in technological change include cost, convenience, usability, accessibility (to all), politics and standardisation.

Standardisation is important because technologies that conform to commonly accepted standards can be used much more widely than those that do not. One of the drivers of digital mobile telephony within

Europe was to develop a technology with a common standard in different countries. Compare this with fixed-line telephony which, although operating to a common standard in many ways (so users can talk across national boundaries), uses a variety of plugs and sockets in different countries (Figure 10).

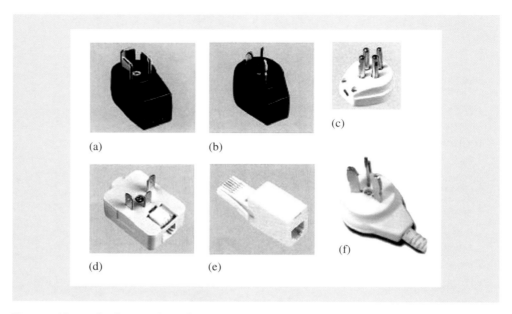

Figure 10 Telephone plugs from various countries: (a) Denmark; (b) Finland; (c) Switzerland; (d) Japan; (e) United Kingdom; (f) Norway

Activity 21 (exploratory)

Take a few moments to think about two entertainment technologies – cinema and audio CD – and what needed to be standardised in order to make them available on a mass scale. Consider, for example, the size of components, the speed of moving components, electrical and optical aspects, etc. When you read my comments, bear in mind that I have brought my own background knowledge to the question, and my list reflects that. I expect your list will be rather different, reflecting your prior knowledge (although I'd be surprised if there are not some common items).

Comment

There are many aspects of standardisation for these technologies. Here are just a few:

Cinema

- width of film strip (8, 16, 35 mm are/were all standards)
- aspect ratio (the ratio of the width and height of the image) which determines the general rectangular shape of the projected image

- speed of projection (24 frames per second for cinema) was standardised in 1927. Note that this is not quite the same as video/television which is 25 frames per second in Europe and 30 frames per second in the USA.
- optical sound recording system (recall Figure 9).

Audio CD

- size of disk
- recording technique for the digital data, including the way the data is represented as microscopic indentations on the disk.

And there are many others in each case, such as electrical standards for power supplies and plugs and sockets. Whatever your list contains, you should appreciate that standards are vital if such technologies are to become widespread. For example, CD players from various manufacturers have to be compatible, as do the projection systems in cinemas nationally, and even internationally. Similar considerations apply to video, CD-ROM, DVD, radio, television, email, computers, and so on. When an agreed standard format does not exist, there are often 'format wars' between competing technologies. The way a particular standard 'wins out' is often a result of a complex mix of technological, social and political effects, as you will see from the following section.

3 A socio-technological case study: video recording

Table 4 lists the chronology of some of the major technical developments in video recording on tape and digital disk. This is a linear story of technological development of the type often given after the event. But it hides a more complex, and much more interesting story.

Table 4   Chronology of main technical developments in video recording

Year	Main technical development
1956	First video recorder, standing nearly 2 m high, recorded 15 minutes on a 20-inch reel of tape, required air conditioning because of the heat generated by the electronic circuits of the time
1957	More 'compact' machine (approx. $1 \times 1 \times 1.5$ m), no air conditioning needed
1967	First Japanese transistorised, colour, reel-to-reel video recorder, retail price around £500 (price of a small car)
1974	Philips (VCR) video cassette recorder introduced
1977	Philips home machine on sale for £600 in UK; one-hour cassette tapes about £20; tape heads had to be replaced every 1000 hours at a cost of £50 Other, incompatible, competing products soon appear on the UK market
1978	Large-format laserdisc introduced, but never achieved huge market success JVC VHS machines with three-hour cassettes launched in the UK
1982	VHS standard emerges as clear winner, three-hour cassettes down to £10
1995	Philips/Sony and Toshiba/Warner announce and demonstrate rival digital disc systems Agreement reached on a common standard for DVD
1996	First DVD players sold in Japan (November)
1997	DVD Forum established (to promote collaboration on future standards development)

First, look at the timescale. Brian Winston (1998), in his book *Media, Technology and Society*, studied a wide range of media technologies, and identified a typical lead time of three or four decades for the establishment of a new technology from early prototypes, and a lot longer from the scientific basis of the technology. This was true for the VCR, and is useful to bear in mind when reading any claim about 'revolutionary' media technologies.

Second, consider one of the key technological developments: the replacement of valves (vacuum tubes) with solid-state (transistorised) electronics. Valves and transistors can both be used in electronic circuits for amplification and other purposes – but there are key differences.

Valves are what are known as 'thermionic devices'; rather like miniature light bulbs, they operate by heating a wire filament to a high temperature. Transistors perform a similar function, but at room temperature; they are based upon solid materials such as silicon – hence the term 'solid state'. The transistor was invented in 1947, but early products using transistors were not particularly successful, or reliable. But because of the transistor's enormous potential to replace the valve in many applications (with the advantages of reduced size, power consumption, and heat generation) huge efforts were devoted over the following decades to improve the technology. Particularly important was the invention of the integrated circuit, in which many transistors and other components were fabricated on a single silicon chip, rather than as individual devices that then had to be interconnected.

But technological improvements were only part of the story.

> The term 'solid state' has also more recently been used to distinguish electronic devices with no moving parts from those that involve some mechanical movement. This is discussed further in Part 2.

Activity 22 (exploratory)

In 1977 a VCR machine cost almost £600, and a young teacher's annual salary was about £3200. By the early twenty-first century, a combined DVD/VCR player could be bought for about £50, and a young teacher earned about £20 000. What can you say about the cost in real terms of VCRs in the late 1970s and DVD players in the early twenty-first century? (Hint: think about the proportion of an average salary needed to buy a player in each case.)

Comment

The early machines cost a fortune – nearly one-fifth or 20% of a young teacher's salary, compared with a mere four-hundredth or so (0.25%) by the early twenty-first century! Running costs in the early days were also high (see Table 4) with expensive tapes and the need to replace recording heads quite frequently.

Standards

Part of the reason for high costs in the late 1970s was the existence of several incompatible standards, the best known of which are VHS (which finally won out) and Sony's Beta (or Betamax) system.

This wasn't necessarily seen as a problem at the time. In 1979 the July *Which?* report stated:

> In the long run, one system may triumph over the others, and become the standard system. But there's no sign of this happening at present. The four existing systems are incompatible – which means that you can't change tapes between systems, though you can still do so between brands using the same system (except that N1500-series VCR [Philips] recorders are also incompatible with N-1700 series VCR-models) [...] But this is unlikely to matter to most people – members didn't often use their video recorders for playing-back pre-recorded tapes, or tapes made on a different machine.
>
> *Which?* (1979)

It's always salutary to look back at old predictions. Just three years after this *Which?* report, VHS was predominant. In fact, the resolution of the incompatibility problem turned out to be one of the key drivers in both the take-up and the development of the technology. Once the VHS system had gained ground at the expense of the other systems, there was far more incentive to purchase a machine. Users did want to swap tapes. Video shops and libraries could invest with confidence in a larger and stable market. Economies of scale meant that manufacturers could lower prices, and different companies competed more vigorously once they all used the same system. Interestingly, the VHS system is sometimes claimed to be inferior in terms of reproduction quality than the Betamax system, and is presented as a rather ironic success story. But whether or not this is true, it misses the point. The success or otherwise of a media technology depends on price, design, marketing, convenience, and many other aspects – the 'whole product – as well as 'technological superiority'. After noting the advice in Activity 23, read what the *Guardian* writer Jack Schofield has to say about the matter.

Activity 23 (self-assessment)

While reading this extract, try to identify the key points the author is making. Highlight them or make notes in the margin. Then write out a list of up to six key points you have identified.

Comment

My answer is given at the end of this part.

WHY VHS WAS BETTER THAN BETAMAX

J. Schofield

25 January 2003

Guardian Unlimited, online.

[...]

'The whole product' model [...] provided a convincing explanation of why VHS had thrashed Betamax. VHS offered a bigger choice of hardware at lower cost, the tapes were cheaper and more easily available, there were a lot more movies to rent, and so on. All of this matched my own experience.

I remember perambulating Hammersmith [...] and finding VHS recorders more readily available to rent, while the video shop had three walls of VHS movies and only one for Betamax.

Indeed, the main thing that didn't fit was the idea that Betamax was 'technically superior'. Standing in a shop at the time, there was absolutely no visible difference in picture quality, and some reviews had found that VHS's quality was superior.

I 'knew' Betamax was superior – that was the received wisdom, even at the time – and maybe it was, in a lab. But I wasn't buying a lab test rig. In terms of 'the whole product', VHS was clearly superior, so that's the way I went. Along with everybody else.

Later I found out that Betamax had owned the market, but lost it because Sony got one simple decision wrong. It chose to make smaller, neater tapes that lasted for an hour, whereas the VHS manufacturers used basically the same technology with a bulkier tape that lasted two hours. Instead of poring over the sound and picture quality, reviewers could simply have taken the systems home. Their spouses/children/grandparents and everybody else would quickly have told them the truth. 'We're going out tonight and I want to record a movie. That Betamax tape is useless: it isn't long enough. Get rid of it.'

Betamax was the first successful consumer video format, and at one time it had close to 100% of the market. All of the video machines in use and all of the pre-recorded movies were Betamax. It had a de facto monopoly, and an element of lock-in (because of tape incompatibilities). It lost because, at the time, it could not do what consumers wanted: record a whole movie unattended. And although Betamax playing times were extended, they never caught up with VHS.

Other elements of the oft-repeated Betamax story are also wrong. For example, while Sony was certainly slow to bring in other manufacturers, it had tried to license it to rivals such as JVC before VHS was even launched. Betamax was not generally more expensive: Sony had to slash its original high prices but generally it was competitive. Indeed, after it had lost the market, Betamax machines were often cheaper than VHS ones.

And at the beginning, there was no comparative shortage of Betamax movies to rent: actually, they were all Betamax. (Stan Liebowitz, Professor and Associate Dean of the School of Management, University of Texas at Dallas, has done most research on this, but see *urbanlegends.com* for a quick guide.)

Even if Betamax had been 'technically superior', it wouldn't have mattered. VHS users have long had the chance to upgrade to the compatible SuperVHS format with superior picture quality. But rather than demanding better pictures for today's TV sets, consumers have shown more interest in LP (Long Play) modes that reduce the picture quality to provide longer recording times.

VHS won because 'the whole product' did what people wanted at a price they were willing to pay. [...]

With the success of the VHS format it became commonplace for friends to meet to watch a video at home, for example; and the desire of people to keep track of favourite serials or soaps while on holiday encouraged manufacturers to add new features, such as timers that allowed several episodes to be recorded automatically, and the 'long play' options already mentioned that gave extra recording time for such purposes. Machines also became available with two tape drives, to enable users to copy tapes. The development of the video recorder is a classic example of the complexities of socio-technical change.

Pornography

Another key influence in the development of the video market appears to have been pornography. Jonathan Coopersmith of Texas A&M University has studied the interrelationship of pornography and technology:

Pornography played a major role in the early years of VCRs by providing customers with a product, and, at the same time, justification for acquiring an expensive piece of equipment. VCR buyers in the late 1970s and early 1980s comprised a new market. Not only was the equipment very costly, but two incompatible formats, VHS and Beta, were jousting for market superiority, so users had to risk buying a format that might soon disappear. Consequently, early VCR buyers were an audience willing to pay a premium for equipment in exchange for the prestige of 'cutting edge' technophiles and also for enjoying viewing privacy.

The VCR created a vast market for pornographic video cassettes world wide. Casual observations of the spread of VCRs in the United States, Britain, Australia and the former Soviet Union revealed that videoporn, much of it American, comprised a large percentage of available tapes in those early years. The German market for adapters to enable PAL-format VCRs to play American NTSC-format video cassettes was fuelled initially by pornography.

> Pornography generated the profits that enticed stores to offer video cassettes. General releases were not put on video until 1978, one year after sexually explicit films. By 1990 pornography trailed only new releases and children's tapes in popularity nationwide and, in the Northeast and West Coast, was second only to new releases.
>
> Coopersmith (1998)

Particularly interesting is Coopersmith's remark about the role of pornography in the development of an adapter to convert between the PAL (UK, Germany and elsewhere) and NTSC (North America and Japan) TV standards. Elsewhere in his article Coopersmith also points out that there was nothing unique about the association of this particular media technology with pornography: the early days of print, photography, film and cable TV were also characterised by close links with pornography – as is, of course, the internet. In fact, it has been argued that many of the commercial features of the Web (advertising, payment, pop-ups, etc.) appeared first in the pornography sector.

Well, you'll find lots of different explanations for the outcome of the 'video wars'. No single explanation is likely to be the full story. What is important is the complexity of what happened, and the way technology, society and markets interacted.

The development of the DVD offers an interesting comparison with the VCR. The idea of a disk, rather like an audio CD but with a vastly increased capacity capable of storing a whole movie, came out of an informal Hollywood committee in 1994. By the following year, two competing systems had been proposed, but unlike the VCR experience the relevant manufacturers agreed on a common standard before launching their products. Perhaps they'd learnt the lessons of the VCR experience! First discussions were acrimonious, but the two competing designs were brought together as a compromise, in part at least because of actions by the major software and hardware giants, who put pressure on the original companies and joined a consortium to develop a common standard. Although the road to standardisation was not easy, and a good deal of bickering and jostling for position took place for some years, the result was a technology that introduced a number of novel coding techniques and gained a market share much more rapidly than was the norm (although DVD technology is firmly based on CD technology and standards for digital television that date from the early 1980s).

The pre-competition standardisation of the video and audio aspects of the DVD was not, however, repeated when it came to recordable and rewritable disks, and the next generation of higher-capacity disks. Here,

a number of competing and incompatible formats were developed. (By the time you read this, the problem may have been resolved, but it was certainly a problem in the earlier days of this technology.)

Like other digital technologies, a major factor in the success of the DVD is the enormous processing power in the player, which can not only cope with the complex procedures needed to recover the original data, but also offer interactivity, multiple sound tracks and many other features.

4 Dealing with the data mountain: compression

One common feature of the emergence of new technologies is that developments may be held up owing to one particular, serious, technological problem. A good example was the need to develop new techniques to cope with the large data files produced by the digital encoding of sound, images, and – in particular – moving pictures. The advantages of digital techniques were recognised several decades ago, but for a long time it was impossible to process and transmit data fast enough for digital television or cinema – or even to store the information in an easily accessible form. Enormous commercial and governmental resources were devoted to solving this problem, often on an international scale. For example, the Joint Photographic Experts Group (JPEG) and the Motion Picture Experts Group (MPEG) were set up to look at systems for the digital coding of still and moving pictures. And in the telecommunications sector, the European Union was a major force in developing the Global System for Mobile (GSM) communications standard for digital mobile phones.

One of the most important technological developments that have helped overcome the obstacle of the data mountain is what is known as **data compression**. Compression means taking the original digital file (representing audio, video, text, etc.) and converting it into a new file that uses considerably fewer bits without significantly degrading the quality. In this section we'll look at a few common techniques used for entertainment applications and elsewhere.

data compression

There's a common pattern to these compression techniques, illustrated in Figure 11. First the source data is analysed, to determine its properties, and how these can be exploited to reduce the size of the file. Following such compression the file is stored or transmitted. And finally, when we want to recover the data, there is a **decompression** process, which reverses the compression.

decompression

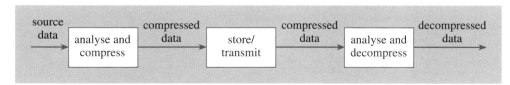

Figure 11   Data compression/decompression

4.1 Runlength encoding

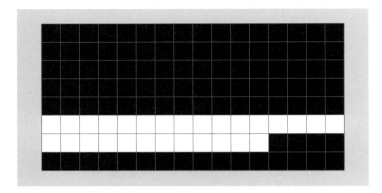

Figure 12 Black and white pattern

Imagine that we need to transmit the black-and-white pattern of Figure 12 encoded as:

1111111111111111

1111111111111111

1111111111111111

1111111111111111

1111111111111111

0000000000000000

0000000000001111

1111111111111111

Rewriting this as a continuous string of binary digits, reading horizontally from top left to bottom right, we have

11111111111111111111111111111111111111111111111111111111111111111111
1111111111111111111111111110000000000000000000000000
00111111111111111111111

– in other words, the sequence

80 ones

28 zeros

20 ones

**runlength
encoding**

One compression technique, called **runlength encoding**, exploits situations like these by transmitting or storing information about the length of 'runs' of ones and zeros, rather than each bit.

So, for example, we might transmit or store a binary coded representation of

```
80(1)28(0)20(1)
```

where 80(1) means a run of 80 ones, 28(0) means a run of 28 zeros, and so on.

There are a number of different systems in use. For example, the above scheme could be made more efficient by beginning with a code (a 'header') to specify whether to start with binary ones or zeros, and then just listing the numbers of ones and zeros:

```
header, 80, 28, 20
```

Two common applications of runlength encoding are:

1   Fax machines. Runlength encoding is ideal, because a typical printed text contains long runs of both white and black pixels. Both black and white pixels are runlength encoded where appropriate, using special codes for the various runs.

2   The JPEG standard for digitising images, widely used in digital still and video cameras. The data is first processed in a way that results in a data file containing a lot of zeros (a result of suppressing information that is unimportant for human perception). This file is then compressed using a version of runlength encoding that codes non-zero values directly, but looks for runs of zeros.

> In these examples I've used brackets and commas simply in order to make clear the principles of what is happening. In practical applications of runlength coding other techniques are used to indicate the length of runs.

Activity 24 (exploratory)

Figure 13 shows a striped pattern, encoded as

```
0101010101010101
0101010101010101
0101010101010101
0101010101010101
0101010101010101
0101010101010101
0101010101010101
0101010101010101
```

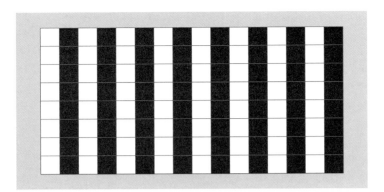

Figure 13 Striped pattern

Would runlength coding as described above result in compression? If not, can you suggest a modification?

Comment

The first runlength scheme above would lead to

    1(0)1(1)1(0)1(1)1(0) ...

Far from compressing the original data, this scheme would mean several bits being transmitted for each original single bit!

The second scheme would lead to

    header, 1, 1, 1, 1, 1, ...

which would increase the file size by a small amount depending on the nature of the header.

Looking at the original pattern, however, we see it is simply 01 repeated 64 times. So a modified coding scheme scanning from top left to bottom right would simply be

    64(01)

which is potentially a huge compression, particularly if the pattern is to be generated on a whole computer screen rather than in my artificial 16×8 format!

You might also have suggested scanning in a different way – a vertical scanning scheme would pick up runs of ones and zeros, in contrast to a horizontal technique. But then extra information would have to be included about which way to scan, something that would also add an overhead.

The important point to note here is that the characteristics of the original data source are vital in deciding exactly what sort of compression to use. In the compression schemes used in current audio, image and video encoding, the original data is analysed in various ways in order to code the data most efficiently.

The runlength coding outlined above is an example of **lossless compression**. In lossless compression, none of the original information is lost: it is possible to reconstruct the original data file perfectly, bit by bit. An alternative approach to data compression is called 'lossy'. In **lossy compression**, the original file is processed in a way that preserves the important information, but discards other information that is less important for the particular application. The original data file cannot be reconstructed perfectly, but if the compression is done appropriately, the reconstructed version will be fit for purpose. The first stage of JPEG, which results in a data file containing a lot of zeros, is lossy compression, but still leads to a final image of acceptable quality.

Various lossy techniques are used in image coding, as you will see later.

lossless compression

lossy compression

4.2   Dictionary-based coding

A very powerful form of lossless coding is called **dictionary-based coding**. An example of such coding is the widely used 'Lempel-Zev-Welch', or LZW algorithm, found in the popular Winzip® compression software, and also in the GIF format used for images in websites.

dictionary-based coding

One way of understanding the basic principles of the LZW algorithm is to consider the compression of text, although the principles can be applied to any data file; the type of file is irrelevant for this type of compression. The basic technique is to analyse the data file for repeated patterns, then use a shorter code to represent each pattern that occurs a number of times. This can be done automatically, building up a 'dictionary' of patterns as the file is examined. Let's have a look at how this can be done. We'll assume that the codes are numbers, representing longer segments of alphabetical text. In practice, the LZW algorithm works directly on binary data, looking for repeated patterns, and representing them by code words.

Activity 25 (self-assessment)

Actually, I sneaked in a suggestion of dictionary-based coding in my discussion of runlength encoding in the last subsection. Can you think what it was?

Comment

The answer is given at the end of this part.

But to get back to dictionary-based coding proper, here's a short extract from a speech by Winston Churchill (delivered at Harrow on 29 October 1941):

> **Do not let us speak of darker days; let us rather speak of sterner days. These are not dark days: these are great days – the greatest days our country has ever lived.**

Looking for repeated patterns in the first sentence, we could begin to build up a dictionary as follows:

Code	Word(s)
1	let us
2	speak of
3	days

We can now replace some of the words by the codes (numbers) that represent them, so the first sentence is encoded as:

> **Do not 1 2 darker 3; 1 rather 2 sterner 3.**

Moving on now to the rest of the quotation, we could extend our dictionary:

Code	Word(s)
1	let us
2	speak of
3	days
4	dark
5	these are
6	great

The whole quotation can then be represented as:

> **Do not 1 2 4er 3; 1 rather 2 sterner 3. 5 not 4 3: 5 6 3 – the 6est 3 our country has ever lived.**

Now, when we store or transmit this coded form, we also have to store or transmit the dictionary along with the code. In short texts, this does not result in a significant compression, since the need to send the dictionary adds a significant overhead. But with longer texts, we tend to find many more repeated words (or letter groupings), and the compression can be much greater, so the need to send the dictionary is not a problem.

So, to summarise, the LZW format operates on binary codes of any type of source file. In essence, the process is:

- look for repeated binary patterns
- build up a 'dictionary' of codes that represent the original, longer repeating binary patterns using fewer bits
- update and modify this 'dictionary' as the file is processed
- select the dictionary codes in a way that makes the compression efficient – for example, the most commonly occurring patterns are allocated shorter binary codes.

Activity 26 (self-assessment)

Now try coding this short extract from a poem by Wendy Cope (1992) by suggesting a dictionary and then encoding the extract:

> **I am a poet.**
>
> **I am very fond of bananas.**
>
> **I am bananas.**
>
> **I am very fond of a poet.**
>
> **I am a poet of bananas.**
>
> **I am very fond.**

Comment

My answer is given at the end of this part.

This discussion has indicated only the broad principles of this type of coding, and shouldn't be taken too literally. For example, in the coding of text we need to include things like upper- and lower-case letters, spaces, punctuation marks, fonts, etc. When the compression algorithm operates on binary files, all these aspects are represented in the binary code, and are taken into account in the selection of recurring binary patterns.

Now would be a good time to attempt the computer activities in Part 3, Section 4, which deal with image coding and file compression, although you may choose to wait until a more convenient time.

4.3 Perceptual coding

perceptual coding

An important class of *lossy* coding is known as **perceptual coding**. Perceptual coding schemes use the power of digital processing to exploit the nature of human hearing and vision. In this way, enormous compression can be achieved in comparison with the sort of digital coding that does not take perception into account. In contrast to the LZW algorithm, which treats all binary files identically, in perceptual coding the nature of the source information is very important in the way the binary code is created.

Activity 27 (self-assessment)

Before reading on, write down a few notes (perhaps in the margin) to explain the difference between lossless and lossy compression.

Comment

My answer is given at the end of this part.

MPEG

Examples of perceptual coding techniques can be found in the **MPEG** set of standards, developed by the Motion Picture Experts Group. These have become some of the most important standards in the entertainment industry. They cover both audio (including the MP3 format used in digital players) and video (digital television as well as movies). In this section I'll introduce some of their most important features.

Audio coding

Let's look first at audio coding. The nature of human hearing has always been an important factor in the technologies of sound recording and reproduction. For example, the range of frequencies (high and low notes) that humans can hear is restricted. So in any audio recording technique there is no point trying to record sounds outside this frequency range. Analogue audio recording and transmission techniques have always restricted the frequency range to one that is considered to be 'good enough'.

'Good enough' is an important criterion, and differs between applications. The quality of sound on a telephone, for example, is good enough for understanding voices easily, but is not considered adequate for music (although in the early days of telephony there were a number of systems in various countries for broadcasting concerts by telephone – 'quality' is relative, and novelty is also an important consideration!) The quality of mobile telephony is sometimes significantly worse than that of land lines, but is acceptable because of the convenience of a mobile. Decisions on what exactly is 'good enough' and 'acceptable' for a given application are taken with the aid of panels of users, who grade the different possibilities during the development of the technologies.

Digital technology has made available a much wider range of possibilities for audio coding than simply restricting the range of frequencies. The next paragraph explains one technique used in MP3 audio files and digital broadcasting.

Humans are much more sensitive to sounds at some frequencies than others. Figure 14 is a graph showing how loud a sound has to be at a particular frequency in order for it to be perceived by a human. The curve is derived from experimental tests on human subjects, in order to obtain an average measure. The details vary widely between individuals – for example, a friend of mine cannot hear bats squeaking when I point it out, but I cannot hear some of the very low sounds made (I am reliably informed by the same friend) by frogs in my garden.

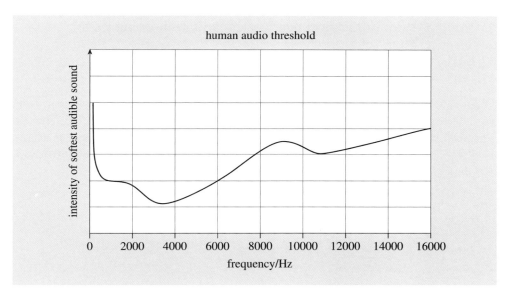

human audio threshold

Figure 14   Relative audio sensitivity of humans

You may come across slightly different versions of this figure, but the general features are the same.

I have labelled the frequency axis of Figure 14 in numerical terms of hertz (Hz), the unit of frequency. (Remember 1 Hz is one cycle per second of a wave – in this case, a sound wave.) I have not labelled the loudness axis with numerical values – it's not worth going into details here of how the loudness of a sound can be quantified, and we're going to be concerned only with the general way the threshold varies with frequency.

Most people can hear only sounds louder than the threshold line shown in Figure 14 for a given frequency. In the MPEG-1 and MPEG-2 standards, designed to be used with multimedia CD-ROMs and digital television, the audio signal is analysed and compared with a graph similar to that shown in Figure 14. Audio content that falls below the threshold for a particular frequency is not coded, since it will not be audible to most listeners.

Activity 28 (self-assessment)

Look again at Figure 14. According to this figure, to what frequencies in the range 1 kHz to 10 kHz is the average human (a) most, and (b) least sensitive?

Comment

My answer is given at the end of this part.

A further complication of human perception is that a loud sound at a particular instant in time affects the shape of Figure 14. A loud sound at one particular frequency decreases the sensitivity of the listener temporarily to other nearby frequencies – so if a particularly loud sound occurs, even more of the rest of the audio signal can be ignored by a recording system (for a short time), because it will not be perceived by the listener. Think of an orchestral concert, for example. If there's a particularly loud brass or percussion part, then some other instruments will hardly be heard for a significant (although short) period of time.

There are a number of other aspects of human perception of sound that are exploited by the MPEG standards. Taken together, they enable a significant compression to be achieved. The popular MP3 format is one option. The MP3 standard can reproduce music that most people find equivalent to CD quality, but using only a fraction of the standard CD bit rate.

In any compression technique there is always a price to be paid. The MPEG audio coding schemes demand highly complex analysis of the audio signal at the recording/transmitting end in order to obtain the desired compression. Players using an MPEG standard also need to process the information quickly in order to reproduce a high-quality version of the original. This requires suitably fast processors at a price consumers are willing to pay. One reason that manufacturers have been willing to invest in the mass production of such complex hardware is market confidence in the MPEG formats.

Image and video coding

Digital image and video coding also exploits aspects of human perception. The next activity asks you a couple of questions to set you thinking. They are a bit open ended, so don't worry if your comments aren't very similar to mine. I'll be explaining more after you have done the activity.

Activity 29 (exploratory)

Here are some facts about image and video recording:

(a) Human perception is less sensitive to colour than it is to brightness. Information about colour and brightness can be coded and recorded separately.

(b) In motion pictures (cinema) or video, there is often very little change between one frame and the next, at least during a particular scene. So, for example, lips might move slightly, but the head stay still; or a background is the same, while the characters move.

Can you suggest how you might exploit this information in the coding of colour image and video files so as to reduce the file sizes?

Comment

(a) If human perception is less sensitive to colour than it is to light intensity, then it makes sense to use fewer bits to code colour information than are used to code the brightness.

(b) If a video frame changes little from one to the next, then only the changes are important, so information about changes could be recorded/transmitted, rather than a whole image.

Both of these techniques are used in MPEG coding schemes.

Let's look in a bit more detail at the second aspect, called 'motion compensation' in the MPEG standards.

There is a short animation that illustrates MPEG motion compensation on the DVD.

There are three types of individual video frame:

1   Some frames are coded completely independently – so-called I-pictures. I-pictures are used, for example, for the first scene in a video clip, or when a completely new image appears.

2   Some frames are coded by predicting the movement of a particular object in a scene. These are called P-pictures. For example, if an object is moving smoothly between one frame and the next, it is only necessary to transmit information about the motion, rather than coding that small section of the image each time it reaches a new position. If the motion is regular, prediction can be used for several frames ahead with considerable accuracy.

3   Some frames, called B-pictures (the B stands for 'bidirectional'), are obtained from the coded data by interpolation – for example, by

taking an I-picture and a P-picture and generating an intermediate picture by averaging the characteristics of the two. Interpolated frames are constructed at the receiving end on the basis of I and P frames, which means that there is no need to transmit any data for B frames.

The sequence of *decoded* frame types when all is going well is, in the European standard:

    IBBPBBPBBPBBIBBPBBPB ...

In other words, two B-pictures between consecutive I- or P-pictures, and 12 frames between each I-picture. If, for some reason, this approach does not give good enough quality, then a new I-picture is introduced to start the sequence again.

This is a very basic explanation of some aspects of MPEG video coding. The important point to remember, as with all data compression, is that the characteristics of the source information are analysed, decisions made about the appropriate way to represent it as a string of bits, and then the source data is processed in order to achieve this. As with other types of compression, there is additional processing involved at the receiver to 'undo' the compression. In the case of motion compensation this can result in a significant delay between the reception and the display of the moving image. Such a delay can be important in live TV using MPEG coding, such as interviews, when any delay longer than a fraction of a second can result in practical problems of maintaining a conversation.

So far, we've considered some aspects of audio and video, but without detailed examination of the coding of still photo images (although these are implicit in video encoding). One of the most important standards for photo image coding (also used as part of MPEG video) is the one produced by the Joint Photographic Experts Group – **JPEG**.

JPEG

If you're a user of a digital camera (or have already carried out this block's computer activities on image formats, in Part 3, Section 4), you'll be aware of JPEG files (file extension .jpg). Just as we can remove or reduce some frequencies in an audio file because they're not important for human hearing, we can process images in a similar way and remove or reduce some components because they're not important for human vision. Files in JPEG format can often be a small fraction (just a few per cent) of the directly encoded bitmap file without appreciable loss of quality as perceived by most people, as will be clear from the computer activities.

5 The influence of computer game technology

There is a computer session about animation described in Part 3, Section 5. You can do this either before or after studying the section below.

Computer games have had a major effect on the development of ICTs for entertainment, and many of the techniques developed initially for games have been applied elsewhere in the ICT sector – in scientific visualisation and modelling, for example. In this section I want you to read about half of an article describing the contribution of one innovative games company, Id Software. If you want to read the rest, you can locate it through the IEEE online library, to which you have access via the OU Library online journals. (If you choose to do this, don't worry if you find the later sections of the article more difficult to understand than the extracts here.)

Whether or not you play computer games, this extract is of interest because of the general importance of the techniques described. The extract describes and explains some of the ways computer games were influenced by, and influenced, PC development. It's not an easy read, and I don't expect you to understand everything in the article. The journal it's taken from, *IEEE Spectrum*, is the monthly journal sent to every member of the IEEE (the Institute of Electrical and Electronics Engineers based in the USA). So readers are expected to be professional engineers with at least some background in electronics, but not necessarily ICT specialists.

Extracting useful information from an article you don't fully understand is an important skill, and one you'll need to develop for your further studies of ICT. I'll try to guide you through this extract so as to help you in this task. I've divided the extract into several parts. Read the first part now, and then attempt Activities 30 and 31.

THE WIZARDRY OF ID

D. Kushner

August 2002

IEEE Spectrum.

[...] Through its technologically innovative games, Id has had a huge influence on everyday computing, from the high-speed, high-color, and high-resolution graphics cards common in today's PCs to the marshalling of an army of on-line game programmers and players who have helped shape popular culture.

[...]

To bring these games to the consumer PC and establish Id as the market leader required skill at simplifying difficult graphics problems and cunning in exploiting on-going improvements in computer graphics cards, processing power, and memory size.

To date, their games have earned over US $150 million in sales, according to The NPD Group, a New York City market research firm.

IT ALL BEGAN WITH A GUY NAMED MARIO

The company owes much of its success to advances made by John Carmack, its 31-year-old lead programmer and cofounder who has been programming games since he was a teenager.

Back in the late 1980s, the electronic gaming industry was dominated by dedicated video game consoles. Most game software was distributed in cartridges, which slotted into the consoles, and as a consequence, writing games required expensive development systems and corporate backing.

The only alternative was home computer game programming, an underworld in which amateurs could develop and distribute software. Writing games for the low-powered machines required only programming skill and a love of gaming.

Four guys with that passion were artist Adrian Carmack; programmer John Carmack (no relation); game designer Tom Hall; and programmer John Romero. While working together at Softdisk (Shreveport, La.), a small software publisher, these inveterate gamers began moonlighting on their own titles.

At the time, the PC was still largely viewed as being for business only. It had, after all, only a handful of screen colors and squeaked out sounds through a tiny tinny speaker. Nonetheless, the Softdisk gamers figured this was enough to start using the PC as a games platform.

First, they decided to see if they could recreate on a PC the gaming industry's biggest hit at the time, Super Mario Brothers 3. This two-dimensional game ran on the Super Nintendo Entertainment System, which drove a regular television screen. The object was to make a moustached plumber, named Mario, leap over platforms and dodge hazards while running across a

landscape below a blue sky strewn with puffy clouds. As Mario ran, the terrain scrolled from side to side to keep him more or less in the middle of the screen. To get the graphics performance required, the Nintendo console resorted to dedicated hardware. 'We had clear examples of console games [like Mario] that did smooth scrolling,' John Carmack says, 'but [in 1990] no one had done it on an IBM PC.'

Activity 30 (self-assessment)

I introduced the symbol '...' earlier and you'll have found it again in this extract. What does it mean?

Comment

My answer is given at the end of this part.

When you quote other people's work, you may wish to leave bits out. If you do, there are two golden rules for academic writing:

1   Every time you leave anything out, however small, use the ellipsis convention.

2   Never delete anything that means that your quotation substantially changes the meaning of the original. For example, suppose that a film review stated: 'Apart from the occasional high points of sheer cinematographic brilliance, the overall impression was pretty second rate.' What would you think of publicity for the film that included the quotation 'sheer cinematographic brilliance' out of context? (Next time you look at a film poster or DVD cover, think about this!)

Activity 31 (exploratory)

How would you describe, in your own words, the content of this first part of the article? Try making yourself a mindmap or a set of brief notes.

I felt that it fell naturally into three main sections. Do you agree?

Comment

First, there's a brief introduction to the company; then the major players are introduced; and finally a technological problem is outlined – how to get games such as *Super Mario Brothers 3* to run on a PC, rather than just a dedicated games console.

It is quite common for a technical article at this level – that is, in a journal aimed at engineers with a wide variety of backgrounds – to start with some fairly accessibly background material, and then to increase the technical content quite rapidly, as you'll see in a moment.

Now read the second part of the article, and indicate in some way (highlighting, marginal notes, etc.) the portions that relate explicitly to the ways that John Carmack managed to speed up the PC version of the game.

You will need to know that graphics cards are plug-in PC components that control the computer display. As PCs developed during the 1980s, increasingly powerful graphics cards were developed to improve display quality. Don't worry if there are other terms you don't fully understand or have not met before.

After a few nights of experimentation, Carmack figured out how to emulate the side-scrolling action on a PC. In the game, the screen image was drawn, or rendered, by assembling an array of 16-by-16-pixel tiles. Usually the on-screen background took over 200 of these square tiles, a blue sky tile here, a cloud tile there, and so on. Graphics for active elements, such as Mario, were then drawn on top of the background.

Any attempt to redraw the entire background every frame resulted in a game that ran too slowly, so Carmack figured out how to have to redraw only a handful of tiles every frame, speeding the game up immensely. His technique relied on a new type of graphics card that had become available, and the observation that the player's movement occurred incrementally, so most of the next frame's scenery had already been drawn.

The new graphics cards were known as Enhanced Graphics Adapter (EGA) cards. They had more on-board video memory than the earlier Color Graphics Adapter (CGA) cards and could display 16 colors at once, instead of four. For Carmack, the extra memory had two important consequences. First, while intended for a single relatively high-resolution screen image, the card's memory could hold several video screens' worth of low-resolution images, typically 300 by 200 pixels, simultaneously, good enough for video games. By pointing to different video memory addresses, the card could switch which image was being sent to the screen at around 60 times a second, allowing smooth animation without annoying flicker. Second, the card could move data around in its video memory much faster than image data could be copied from the PC's main memory to the card, eliminating a major graphics performance bottleneck.

Carmack wrote a so-called graphics display engine that exploited both properties to the full by using a technique that had been originally developed in the 1970s for scrolling over large images, such as satellite photographs. First, he assembled a complete screen in video memory, tile by tile – plus a border one tile wide [Figure 15].

If the player moved one pixel in any direction, the display engine moved the origin of the image it sent to the screen by one pixel in the corresponding direction. No new tiles had to be drawn. When the player's movements finally pushed the screen image to the outer edge of a border, the engine still did not redraw most of the screen. Instead, it copied most of the existing image – the part that would remain constant – into another portion of video memory. Then it added the new tiles and moved the origin of the screen display so that it pointed to the new image.

In short, rather than having the PC redraw tens of thousands of pixels every time the player moved, the engine usually had to change only a single

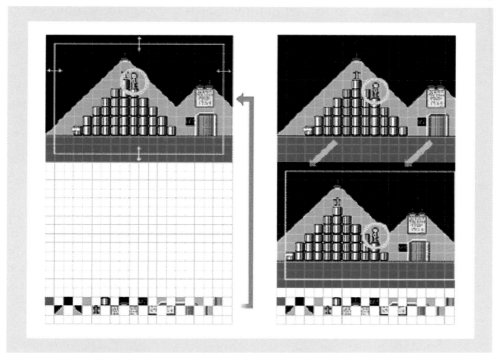

Figure 15   Scrolling with the action. For two-dimensional scrolling in his PC game, programmer John Carmack cheated a little by not always redrawing the background. He built the background of graphical tiles stored in video memory (left) but only sent part of the image to the screen (top left, inside orange border). As the play character (yellow circle) moved, the background sent to the screen was adjusted to include tiles outside the border (see top right). New background elements would be needed only after a shift of one tile width. Then, most of the background was copied to another region of video memory (see bottom right), and the screen image centred in the new background

memory address – the one that indicated the origin of the screen image – or, at worst, draw a relatively thin strip of pixels for the new tiles. So the PC's CPU was left with plenty of time for other tasks, such as drawing and animating the game's moving platforms, hostile characters, and the other active elements with which the player interacted.

Don't read on until you've attempted Activity 32.

Activity 32 (exploratory)

In your own words, write a few sentences about how Carmack managed to speed up the scrolling. Think about the keywords 'speed', 'memory' and 'image updating'.

Comment

Carmack exploited the increased memory of the new EGA video cards. He used the memory to hold several low-resolution images, rather than the single high-resolution one for which the card had been designed. These low-resolution images could be sent to the screen very quickly, resulting in smooth animation.

Carmack wrote some graphics software that enabled rapid scrolling. The screen background, plus an extra 'border' area, was held in the graphics card memory. When a player moved, the area actually displayed on screen was just adjusted slightly. Most of the time there was no need to draw any new background.

Now read the third and final part of this extract. This time, concentrate on the technique known as raycasting. Again, don't worry about terms you've not met, and don't expect to understand everything. (If you've not met the terms polygon and trapezoid, in this context they simply refer to the way rectangles appear from a particular perspective.)

[Carmack] had been experimenting with 3-D graphics ever since junior high school, when he produced wire-frame MTV logos on his Apple II. Since then, several game creators had experimented with first-person 3-D points of view, where the flat tiles of 2-D games are replaced by polygons forming the surfaces of the player's surrounding environment. The player no longer felt outside, looking in on the game's world, but saw it as if from the inside.

The results had been mixed, though. The PC was simply too slow to redraw detailed 3-D scenes as the player's position shifted. It had to draw lots of surfaces for each and every frame sent to the screen, including many that would be obscured by other surfaces closer to the player.

Carmack had an idea that would let the computer draw only those surfaces that were seen by the player. 'If you're willing to restrict the flexibility of your approach,' he says, 'you can almost always do something better.'

So he chose not to address the general problem of drawing arbitrary polygons that could be positioned anywhere in space, but designed a program that would draw only trapezoids. His concern at this time was with walls (which are shaped like trapezoids in 3-D), not ceilings or floors.

For his program, Carmack simplified a technique for rendering realistic images on then high-end systems. In raycasting, as it is called, the computer draws scenes by extending lines from the player's position in the direction he or she is facing. When it strikes a surface, the pixel corresponding to that line on the player's screen is painted the appropriate color. None of the computer's time is wasted on drawing surfaces that would never be seen anyway. By only drawing walls, Carmack could raycast scenes very quickly.

Carmack's final challenge was to furnish his 3-D world with treasure chests, hostile characters, and other objects. Once again, he simplified the task, this time by using 2-D graphical icons, known as sprites. He got the computer to

scale the size of the sprite, depending on the player's location, so that he did not have to model the objects as 3-D figures, a task that would have slowed the game painfully. By combining sprites with raycasting, Carmack was able to place players in a fast-moving 3-D world. The upshot was Hovertank, released in April 1991. It was the first fast-action 3-D first-person action shooter for the PC.

[...]

INSTANT SENSATION

For Id's next game, Wolfenstein 3D, Carmack refined his code. A key decision ensured the graphics engine had as little work to do as possible: to make the walls even easier to draw, they would all be the same height.

This speeded up raycasting immensely. In normal raycasting, one line is projected through space for every pixel displayed. A 320-by-200-pixel screen image of the type common at the time required 64 000 lines. But because Carmack's walls were uniform from top to bottom, he had to raycast along only one horizontal plane, just 320 lines [Figure 16].

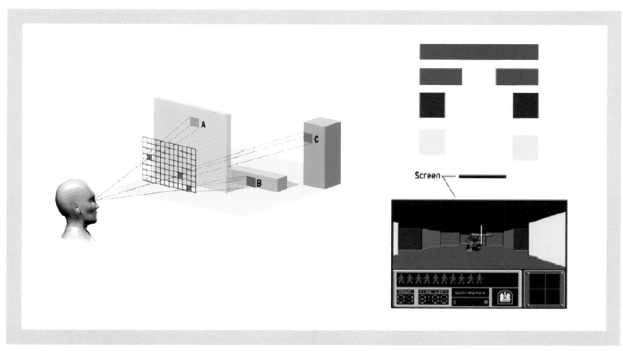

Figure 16 Raycasting 3-D rooms. To quickly draw three-dimensional rooms without drawing obscured and thus unnecessary surfaces, Carmack used a simplified form of raycasting, a technique used to create realistic 3-D images. In raycasting, the computer draws scenes by extending lines from the player's viewpoint (left), through an imaginary grid, so that they strike the surfaces the player sees; only these surfaces get drawn. Carmack simplified things by keeping all the walls the same height. This allowed him to extend the rays from the player in just a single horizontal 2-D plan (top right) and scale the apparent height of the wall according to its distance from the player, instead of determining every point on the wall individually. The result is the final 3-D image of the walls (bottom right)

[...]

By this time, Carmack was programming for the Video Graphics Adapter (VGA) cards that had supplanted the EGA cards. VGA allowed 256 colors – a big step up from EGA's 16, but still a limited range that made it a challenge to incorporate all the shading needed for diminished lighting effects.

The solution was to restrict the palette used for the game's graphics, so that 16 shades of each of 16 colors could be accommodated. Carmack then programmed the computer to display different shades based on the player's location within a room. The darkest hues of a color were applied to far sections of a room; nearer surfaces would always be brighter than those farther away. This added to the moody atmosphere of the game.

Activity 33 (exploratory)

(a) What is raycasting? How did Carmack simplify the technique?

(b) How did Carmack obtain sufficient shades to produce an adequate display of the gaming environment?

Comment

(a) Raycasting is a technique for identifying which parts of a three-dimensional scene can be viewed by an observer at a particular point. Imaginary rays are 'drawn' from the observer to the scene. Only the surfaces that are visible to the observer are drawn on the screen, reducing the load on the computer. Carmack simplified this technique by using a 3-D environment in which all the walls were of the same height. This meant that the number of rays required could be drastically reduced.

(b) Carmack restricted the number of colours to 16 (the VGA allowed 256), but each of those was available in 16 shades, using up the $16 \times 16 = 256$ possibilities. So although the colour variation was limited, there was a wide range of shades available to simulate depth in the image.

Activity 34 (exploratory)

Spend a few minutes reviewing your work on this extract, including your responses to Activities 31–33. Given my comments on the activities, how satisfied were you with your answers? Did you find parts of the extracts difficult to understand? If so, which?

Comment

I said at the beginning of this section that this article was not an easy read! When I first chose it for T175, I found the discussion of both the scrolling and the raycasting quite hard going. I didn't think the figures were always particularly helpful, either.

Unfortunately, if you're to study any subject seriously at university level, you'll need to develop strategies to cope with material you don't fully understand. Part of such a strategy is to accept that even without fully understanding a text, you'll be able to extract important information.

Some strategies you can use to deal with a difficult text are:

- Pose yourself one or two questions, rather like the questions I asked in Activities 31–33, and bear these questions in mind as you read.

- Highlight important sentences or passages, or make marginal notes as you go along.

- Write short summaries in response to your own questions.

- If you don't understand a section, try to decide whether it is important. If it is, go back to it; but if it is not important for the task in hand, just accept that you do not (fully) understand it.

My comments after each activity illustrate what I hope you have been able to glean from this extract, so if you've managed a reasonable proportion of what I've written there (in your own words, of course), you've achieved what I hoped from this exercise.

6 Summary of Block 3 Part 1

This part of Block 3 has introduced you to various technical aspects of the use of ICTs in the entertainment context, as well as to some of the wider socio-technological implications of such technologies.

You have been introduced to the basic principles of coding sound and images in digital form, and to ways of coping with the vast amounts of data that can result. Data compression is a particularly important technique used in entertainment technologies and elsewhere. A number of common compression techniques exploit the nature of human perception. For example, many sound and image coding techniques analyse the original signal, and reject elements that will be imperceptible to the majority of listeners or viewers, or are simply not needed for the particular application.

The importance of standards has been stressed, as has the need for an ICT product to be acceptable to the market if it is to succeed – the notion of the 'whole product'. The case study of video recording (both magnetic tape and optical disk technologies) is a salutary reminder of the significance of such aspects.

In the final section of this part you were asked to read a technical article and extract information from it without necessarily fully understanding it. This is an important skill for anyone studying technology, particularly when the pace of change is as rapid as it is for the ICTs.

Answers to self-assessment activities

Activity 6

In an 'analogue' representation, one medium is a direct counterpart of another. A sound signal, for example, can be converted into an electrical 'analogue' and then stored or transmitted. The variations of the electrical 'analogue' show the same pattern of variations as those in the original sound wave. Analogue representations can generally take on any value within a range.

In a 'digital' representation, a limited set of symbols is used to store, transmit, or display a coded version of the original. So a digital representation can have only certain values. Printed text and Morse code are examples of digital representations, as is the numerical display of a digital room thermometer.

Activity 8

Change all the 0s to 1s, and all the 1s to 0s.

Activity 9

(a) For the lower-resolution display we have a total of $800 \times 600 = 480\ 000$ pixels.

For the higher resolution we have $1600 \times 1200 = 1\ 920\ 000$ pixels.

(b) The ratio is $1\ 920\ 000\ /\ 480\ 000 = 4$.

Activity 11

00 becomes 11, so the background changes from white to black.

01 becomes 10, so the left side of the triangle changes from red to blue.

10 becomes 01, so the right side of the triangle changes from blue to red.

11 becomes 00, so the base of the triangle changes from black to white.

Activity 12

We can generate the new words in the same way as before. First, take the previous eight, 3-bit words, and add a binary 0 to the front. Then do the same with a binary 1. Now we have sixteen, 4-bit code words for sixteen different colours, as shown in the margin (I've not tried to think of sixteen colour words!).

You may have written out the binary codes in a different order, but the order given is the standard way of doing this, and includes all possible codes for 4-bit words.

0000	1000
0001	1001
0010	1010
0011	1011
0100	1100
0101	1101
0110	1110
0111	1111

Activity 14

Looking back at Table 2 we see that 8-bit words can represent only 256 codes, while 9-bit words offer 512. So we'd have to use 9-bit words, but we'd need only 300 out of the 512 codes.

Activity 15

(a) $1024 \times 768 = 786\ 432$ pixels. So if each pixel needs 24 bits for the colour information, a complete image requires $786\ 432 \times 24 = 18\ 874\ 368$ bits.

(b) Downloading time for the modem would be $18\ 874\ 368/44\ 000 = 429$ s (to the nearest second). In minutes that's $429/60$ – just over 7 minutes.

(c) For the broadband connection it would be $18\ 874\ 368/512\ 000 = 37$ s (to the nearest second).

(d) 3 Mbps equals 3000 kpbs, so in this example the DVD transfer is nearly six times faster than broadband, so would take around 6 seconds for the image.

Activity 17

The receiver will be able to tell that there has been an error, because the two bits will differ, but it will be impossible to know which is correct. Transmitting each bit twice means that there is $1/2 = 50\%$ redundancy; this compares with 67% redundancy for the triplet example.

Activity 18

It's analogue. The clue is that I said the optical pattern is 'continuously varying' – in effect the proportion of black to white corresponds to the sound intensity at any given time.

Activity 19

(a) The ease of processing once information is in digital form. I mentioned graphics processing, editing, copying, and special effects.

(b) The possibility of error detection and correction. I described 'best-out-of-three' transmission for error correction, and 'transmit twice' for error detection.

(c) Common digital technology for all applications. Examples include audio, video, motion picture, photography, etc., and the rise of the internet as a common delivery medium.

Activity 23

- Whole product model includes a lot more than technology.
- To the average viewer, Betamax did not offer better quality.
- VHS offered longer tapes to record, which was what consumers wanted.
- In the early days expense was not a key issue.
- To start with Betamax offered a wide range of rental cassettes, but later VHS had a much greater range.
- Functions like 'long play' were of more interest to consumers than higher picture quality.

Activity 25

When we looked at the striped pattern of Figure 13, I identified a repeating pattern of 01 that could be coded in such a way.

Activity 26

Clearly there are a lot of repeated words and phrases here, but it's not obvious which choices for dictionary entries would be most efficient. For example, we could choose 'I am' as an entry, or 'I am very fond'. (The remainder of the poem would help us make the choice.) My attempt at this fragment, not necessarily the best, is:

Code	Word(s)
1	I am
2	a poet
3	very fond
4	of
5	bananas

So the coded version (ignoring the full stops) is:

1 2

1 3 4 5

1 5

1 3 4 2

1 2 4 5

1 3

Activity 27

Lossless – no information is lost during compression – we can reconstruct the original file bit by bit.

Lossy – information needed for the particular application is preserved, rest discarded – original file cannot be reconstructed perfectly, but decompressed version is fit for purpose.

Activity 28

The threshold line indicates the quietest sound that can be heard. So the ear is most sensitive where the threshold is lowest, at about 3500 Hz or 3.5 kHz. Similarly, it is least sensitive where the threshold is highest within this range, at about 9 kHz.

Did you identify these correctly? Or did you get them the wrong way round? If you got them wrong, make sure you understand how the threshold line represents the border between audibility and inaudibility – where the threshold line is *lower*, the ear is *most* sensitive.

Activity 30

The three dots are called 'ellipsis', and mean that I have deleted parts of the original article that I felt were not particularly helpful for your study. The square brackets are used to indicate any change from the original when you quote something.

REFERENCES

Coopersmith, J. (1998) 'Pornography, technology and progress', *ICON*, vol. 4, pp. 94–105.

Cope, W. (1992) *Serious Concerns*, London, Faber & Faber.

Kushner, D. (2002) 'The wizardry of Id', *IEEE Spectrum*, vol. 39, no. 8, August, pp. 42–7.

Schofield, J. (2003) *Guardian Unlimited*, 25 January.

Winston, B. (1998) *Media, Technology and Society*, London, Routledge.

Which? (1979) July, p. 417. Consumers' Association, London.

ACKNOWLEDGEMENTS

Grateful acknowledgement is made to the following sources for permission to reproduce material within this book.

Text

Cope W., (1992), 'The Uncertainty of the Poet', *Serious Concerns*, Faber and Faber Limited.

Kushner D., (2002), 'The Wizardry of Id', *IEEE Spectrum*, IEEE Copyrights and Permissions.

Schofield J., (2003), 'Why VHS was better than Betamax', © Guardian Newspapers Limited.

Figures

Figure 9: Ronald Grant Archive.

Figure 10: Images by permission of R. Freshwater.

Part 2
Information

David Chapman

1 Bringing the news on the back of a horse

There is material relevant to this part of Block 3 on the T175 website. Ideally you should look at the online material before studying this part, but if that is not possible you should continue with this part now and look at the online material as soon as convenient.

We seem to be surrounded by 'news' these days, but it was not always like that. On the course website there is a short extract from Shakespeare's *Henry IV Part 2* in which Falstaff hears the news that his former friend and drinking partner, Prince Hal, is now King Henry V, following the death of Henry IV. It is a comic scene set in Gloucestershire, 200 km from the royal court in London, and it is clear that before the messenger (called Pistol) arrived on horseback Falstaff did not even know that Henry IV had died.

It would not be like that now. Maybe Falstaff would have got a text message on his mobile phone:

Hnry 4 ded. Hal 2 b Kng Hnry 5.

And perhaps he would have then dashed home to watch *BBC News 24*, listen to *Radio Five Live* or log on to www.royal.gov.uk.

I do not want to dwell for long on the times before the Industrial Revolution, but before we move on I would like to draw out some of the themes, issues and concepts that help to provide a framework for discussing newsgathering and dissemination of news.

Activity 1 (exploratory)

Think for a moment about the following aspects of news dissemination during the time of Henry IV and V (15th century), or any time before the Industrial Revolution.

(a) What determined how fast the news could get from one place to another?

(b) What determined how much information you could get about an event?

(c) What determined how many people could find out about an event?

(d) How far could news travel?

Comment

For the most part, news would have travelled with people, so the answer to all of the questions about the spread of news is linked with individuals travelling. There were a few other methods that didn't require people to travel, such as beacons, semaphore and carrier pigeons, but these had rather specialised applications.

(a) The fastest means of transport on land would have been a galloping horse, so we can think of news travelling at up to a few tens of kilometres an hour.

(b) If a messenger is bringing the news, then perhaps the amount of information they can carry is determined by how good their memory is. They might also, or instead, have something in writing (exploiting technology) and the text could supplement their memory. Either way, a messenger can bring quite a lot of information.

(c) If the spread of news is relying on word of mouth, then we can imagine news spreading in the way of the 'office grapevine' today, where one person tells two or three others who each tell another two or three people and so on. The total number of people who know the news rises rapidly in this way. Alternatively, if the news is written down, the written text can be passed around and read by more than one person (assuming widespread literacy). Even better, once printing has been invented, large numbers of copies can be produced and many people can read it at the same time.

(d) In principle there is no limit to how far news can travel – it just might take a long time, since the speed at which it travels is limited to that of a galloping horse. In practice, only the most important news items are likely to get very far.

There is an associated computer (spreadsheet) activity in Part 3, Section 3.3, which models the spread of news via the 'office grapevine'. You can do this now, or wait until a more convenient time.

2 From newsreels to real news

With the Industrial Revolution the idea of 'news' developed rapidly, and these days most people in the UK and other developed countries have a concept of 'the news'. We expect to be kept up to date with the news through various sources, and to satisfy this expectation we have the businesses of newsgathering and dissemination of news.

In this section you will be learning about the development of the technologies used for news-gathering and dissemination by reading extracts from a paper written by one of the leading experts in the field.

In 1995 the IEE (Institution of Electrical Engineers – a UK-based association) held a colloquium entitled *Capturing the Action: Changes in Newsgathering*, which brought together technical experts working in the business of newsgathering in order to review developments. The introductory talk at the colloquium was presented by E. V. Taylor, who was at that time Head of Technology at ITN. His talk, 'From newsreels to real news', reviewed developments in news technology from the Industrial Revolution to 1995. As is usual with a colloquium, a 'Colloquium Digest' was produced which contained technical papers associated with each of the talks. I shall be using Taylor's paper to look at the role of ICT in the news business.

> A colloquium is a meeting at which specialists give talks on a topic or on related topics and then lead a discussion about them.

There are two factors which you should bear in mind as you read the paper.

1   The audience was made up of people working in the field or with specific interest in newsgathering. Taylor was able to assume, therefore, that his audience was already familiar with many of the concepts and the specialist language ('jargon') that he used.

2   Although the colloquium digest is available as an IEE publication, its primary distribution was to delegates who attended the colloquium (it would have been given to them when they arrived on the day). It would be used as a reminder of the talk and to fill in some of the factual details that the audience might have missed. It was not produced as a stand-alone document in the form you would find in a journal. There are no section headings, for example, and it is written using language similar to the language Taylor would have used when speaking.

Despite these shortcomings as a stand-alone printed text, Taylor's paper provides an excellent overview of the role of technology in the broadcast news industry, written by an expert who was living through the changes that were taking place. The paper is reproduced verbatim as a resource on the course website, but in the text which follows I have broken it down into a few paragraphs at a time and removed some text not needed for my purposes. I have also added a commentary to explain some of the terms and to discuss some other important topics in ICT.

Taylor's introductory comments

Taylor starts with some introductory comments. Notice the informal style he uses because this is essentially a script for a talk to a colloquium. Notice also the other issue that I raised earlier, that Taylor is assuming that his listeners are familiar with terms such as ITN, ENG and video servers. I shall explain terms like these as we go through the paper. I have highlighted in bold terms which I explain or discuss further in following notes.

From Newsreels To Real News

E.V. Taylor

1995

Institution of Electrical Engineers

Prompted partly by the fact that **ITN** has just celebrated its 40th anniversary, I would like to start by briefly reviewing some of the historical landmarks in news broadcasting that were driven by past technological development.

With this review as a reference I hope I can convince you of the enormous importance of the new technological developments you will hear about today. Make no mistake; for the TV news business these developments are going to create a revolution even greater than that caused by **ENG** in the late 70s/ early 80s – and those of us who lived through that particular revolution still bear some of the scars. So when, very shortly, we have to face the realities of **video servers, digital compression and digital tapeless integrated newsrooms** – make sure your seat belt is pulled nice and tight! We will all need to keep our nerve as I suspect it will be a bumpy ride.

ITN stands for Independent Television News. To quote from the ITN website (ITN, 2005), 'ITN is one of the largest news organisations in the world, producing news and factual programmes for television, radio and new media platforms, both in Britain and overseas. ITN was founded in 1955, as an independent organisation owned by ITV companies producing news programmes for national broadcast on ITV.'

ENG is an abbreviation of Electronic News Gathering. It is the process of recording sound and images electronically, originally as analogue signals on magnetic tapes (video and audio tapes), and conveying them back to the newsrooms in an electronic format; this could be done by physically transporting the tapes or sending the electronic signals over a communications network. ENG is here contrasted with the previous use of film.

Video servers, digital compression and digital tapeless integrated newsrooms. Video servers are computers with large storage capacity (large hard disks or sets of hard disks) used to store and retrieve compressed digital video files. News editors in the 'digital tapeless newsroom' will be working on computers that interface with the server.

Activity 2 (self-assessment)

(a) From your study of Part 1 of this block, explain the purpose of 'digital compression'.

(b) Name one standard that you read about in Part 1 of this block that can be used to compress digital video.

Comment

The answer is given at the end of this part.

Newspapers

Taylor now discusses some early information and communication technologies and the extent to which they had an impact upon newspapers.

So let me start by looking at what was often optimistically called 'news' in the early years of the 20th Century.

Before the establishment of regular radio services in the early 1920s the public were entirely reliant upon the newspaper industry for information about what was going on locally, nationally and internationally.

Despite the development of the telegraph by William Cooke in 1837, and later the telephone by Alexander Graham Bell in 1876, it was really not until the 20th Century that **lines infrastructures** were developed sufficiently for newspapers to be in a position to report the remoter national events in the same week that they occurred. Reporting of events abroad was often many weeks or even months behind the occurrence. Photography had been invented in the 1830s but even by the 1900s newspaper photographs were a rarity and stories were frequently illustrated by sketches, diagrams and cartoons (interesting to note that in the UK at least artists' sketches are still the way we illustrate what is happening within a courtroom where cameras are prohibited). Newspaper photographs did exist of course but had to be hand carried back to the newspaper offices by train, ship or road – a time consuming business in those days.

This situation improved dramatically for the newspaper industry by the development of the **wire picture** by Reuters in the early part of this century. It is worth noting that the Reuter system was a very early example of digital coding and even incorporated data compression with a form of what we now call 'run length coding' – not much is really new, is it? This development enabled pictures to accompany the telegraphed or telephoned reports from many major cities in Europe and the US.

As a consequence, the newspapers prospered and fortunes were made by the now infamous press barons whose influence on both the public and governments was considerable.

*The **lines infrastructure** refers to the network of wires connecting different places together ('line' as in 'telephone line' or 'transmission line').*

*The idea of a **wire picture** is that an image is coded in a method that allows it to be transmitted over 'a wire' – i.e. sent along a telegraph link.*

Taylor highlights the development of the lines infrastructure and invention of the wire picture as being developments that enabled telephony and telegraphy to be exploited by the news industry.

These are two themes you will find coming up all the time in discussions of ICT systems: networking issues – specifically 'network reach' – and coding.

Activity 3 (self-assessment)

How does runlength coding compress binary data? Describe how it works in one or two sentences, based on your study of Part 1 of this block.

Comment

The answer is given at the end of this part.

Radio and newsreels

Taylor compares the merits of radio and newsreels, as sources of news, with those of newspapers.

The value of radio as a communications medium had proved itself during the 1914–18 conflict following its development around the turn of the century by Marconi, Hertz, Popov and others.

The passing of the First World War soon saw the establishment of many national radio broadcasting organisations, the BBC being formed in 1922.

It was not long before regular news bulletins were being broadcast and despite the development of the technique of going over live to quote 'our reporter on the spot', which considerably enhanced the impact of the report, radio was of course not able to illustrate the news.

Despite some imaginative painting of pictures with words, the newspaper industry did not regard radio as a threat but more as a useful advertising medium to alert the public to the fact that something interesting or dramatic had happened causing them to **dash out to buy a newspaper** to get the details and all important pictures to fill in the gaps in the radio report.

During the 1930s the ability to add live action **sound onto film** caused the cinema industry to explode onto the mass entertainment scene. The visual power of cinema as a news medium was quickly recognised and organisations such as British Movietone News and Pathe News soon established themselves with 'newsreels' which were a compilation of the week's best visual stories shot and made on high quality **35 mm film**.

Despite the likelihood of the cinema goers already being aware of the newsreel stories, it was the combination of well-shot pictures with well-written, punchy commentaries which made these newsreels very popular, especially during the Second World War where the visual impact was sometimes quite shocking with audiences unused to the realities of life frequently reduced to tears.

So it had taken around 100 years to develop a means and organisation from the original enabling telegraphic and photographics technologies to deliver moving news images to the public albeit somewhat later than the actual event.

In the meantime, the newspapers continued to be the primary source of news for the public.

*I was struck here by Taylor's comment that the public would '**dash out to buy a newspaper** to get the details and all-important pictures to fill in the gaps in the radio report', because I will still buy a newspaper to get more details about a topic – even if I've seen pictures on TV. This raises the question of how much information you can get from different media (I believe I get more from the newspaper than from a TV report). There are also perhaps differences in the nature of the information that you can get from different media, with more comment and analysis in newspapers.*

*'[T]he ability to add live action **sound onto film**' mentioned by Taylor is significant because there was no sound on early film (as in 'silent movies'), and mechanisms for recording sound onto film alongside the images came later (in the 1930s). The methods used were analogue.*

*The reference to **35 mm** refers to the width of the film. The wider a film, the bigger the picture and the higher the quality of the projected image. However, as Taylor discusses later in the paper, the equipment needed for filming in a narrower width (16 mm was used) was lighter and more portable.*

Activity 4 (exploratory)

From your reading of this material and your understanding of the media, list the merits and limitations of each of: newspaper, radio and newsreels, as a source of news during the 1920s and 1930s. How does today's television news compare?

Comment

Newspaper. Merits: (still) pictures, details of news stories, and you can choose when and at what pace to read. Limitations: delay (not live), no moving images, no sound.

Radio. Merits: live reports, sound. Limitations: no images.

Newsreels. Merits: moving images, sound. Limitations: delay (not live).

Today's television has the merits of radio and newsreels – live reports with sound and moving images – but often not as much depth and analysis as you can get in newspapers, nor does it have the time flexibility of newspapers.

Early television

In the next part of the paper Taylor discusses the early days of television.

This status quo of print/radio/cinema newsreels existed until the early 1950s when the BBC **restarted TV** services [...].

It was natural that news bulletins would form part of this **reborn** visual communications medium. But resources were in short supply and early BBC TV news programmes were little more than radio news read into camera by a newsreader with a posh voice wearing a dinner jacket. What picture they did have was like the cinema newsreels shot on 35mm film.

There was nothing there to threaten the newspaper proprietors.

But in 1955 came Commercial Television and the creation of Independent Television News.

From the start, ITN wanted to produce a newscast which would be different from the BBC's by showing much more moving picture.

Here technology came to the aid of ITN. Recent improvements had been made to the quality of film stock and ITN took **the then controversial decision to adopt 16mm film**.

Compared with 35mm equipment, the 16mm camera was very light, more manageable and much more affordable to purchase and operate. It was therefore more suitable for volume newsgathering.

ITN judged, quite correctly as it turned out, that illustrating more stories with moving pictures would appeal to the public – even if the picture quality was somewhat worse than they were used to in the cinema or on the BBC.

The BBC soon followed with its own 16mm equipped film crews.

[...]

By the end of the 1960s, with the introduction of colour, bulletins were taking on a style not too far removed from present day news bulletins – remember the first broadcast of News At Ten, the first half-hour news on British TV, which was in 1967.

Something else happened in the latter half of the 1960s which was to have a major impact on the immediacy of TV news – the development of the **communications satellite**.

Telstar in 1962 had shown the way ahead and was rapidly followed by the **geostationary** Early Bird satellites over the Atlantic Ocean.

TV news companies were now able to include live reports from the USA in their news bulletins.

By the early 1970s the satellite networks had become global and TV news companies were regularly including illustrated stories from around the world into their evening news programmes despite the very high price tag of $2,000 for a 10 minute slot.

The newspaper industry was now beginning to worry – television news was able to include stories in late evening bulletins which the dailies did not have for their next day editions.

Restarted TV ... reborn. The BBC started a TV service in 1936, but it was suspended at the outbreak of the Second World War in 1939. It was restarted after the end of the war.

The then controversial decision to adopt 16mm film. Taylor here explains how the lower quality of 16 mm film compared with 35 mm film was more than offset by other advantages of using the smaller format.

There are parallels here in other ICT contexts, where the balance between quality and 'being able to do it at all' leans towards the 'being able to do it'. For example, people seem to be willing to accept inferior sound quality from mobile telephones compared with fixed-line phones.

To put it another way, 'good enough' wins over 'the best', and in general, digital techniques allow you to make trade-offs so that the quality is pitched at 'good enough' for any given service. In digital audio broadcasting (DAB, digital radio) a trade-off is possible between the number of channels available and the sound quality. Currently, DAB uses a much lower quality than possible to allow for a large number of channels.

Communications satellites. Orbit the Earth and allow communications by microwave links between terrestrial locations that are a long way apart (Figure 1). They can be used for communications between fixed locations on the Earth or else to provide a wide coverage for mobile users. The original use was only for fixed locations, because the ground stations (the transmitting and receiving aerials and associated equipment on the Earth) needed for the users on the Earth were too large to be mobile.

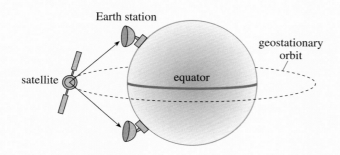

Figure 1 Communications satellite

Satellites have to be orbiting in order to stay at a fixed height above the Earth, and the speed at which they orbit is related to their height. The higher they are, the longer they take to go once around the Earth. At one particular height – about 36 000 km above the ground – the orbit time is 24 hours. If a satellite's orbit is a ring directly above the equator at this height, the satellite will remain over the same spot on Earth. Such an orbit is known as a geostationary orbit, and a satellite in a geostationary orbit is called a **geostationary satellite**.

Telstar I was the first communications satellite that allowed television signals to be sent across the Atlantic, in 1962. Telstar I was not in a geostationary orbit and as a consequence was only in the right position to allow transatlantic communications for 30 minutes at a time, three or four times a day.

geostationary satellite

Activity 5 (self-assessment)

What are the advantages of using 16 mm film that offset its poorer quality compared with 35 mm?

Comment

The answer is given at the end of this part.

From film to videotapes

Taylor now describes the era when film was replaced with analogue electrical video.

However, despite all these electronic advances, our newsgathering was still all film based – but the next development was not too far away.

In 1976 **RCA** demonstrated the [...] '**Hawkeye**' combined camera and recorder as an all electronic concept to replace newsfilm.

This development sparked the imagination of news broadcasters who quickly recognised the benefits of getting away from film with all its processing delays and bulky, expensive **telecine** equipment and of course its inability to provide live coverage.

By 1979 the ENG revolution was gathering momentum and it soon became unstoppable.

In 1980 ITN became the first UK broadcaster to introduce large scale ENG operations. By 1982 film as a newsgathering medium was dead.

TV news was now moving into the position of being the public's primary source of news, with newspapers accepting that they had lost the battle.

It had taken TV news just 30 years from its inception to reach this dominant position. The news reels of the 1930s, 1940s and 1950s were long gone and the demand for real up to the minute news was growing even stronger.

Well, there were still large areas of the world which did not have a **wideband cable** infrastructure or possess large expensive satellite ground stations and these became the next technological battleground.

These **communication dead spots** provided the challenge to fire the development of transportable ground stations.

In 1985 ITN formed an alliance with the **IBA** and McMichael Electronics to develop the world's first **SNG uplinks** – the **Newshawk** – which we first used in 1986.

[...]

RCA (which originally stood for Radio Corporation of America) is the company that manufactured the equipment it called '**Hawkeye**', which was one of the first examples of what we now call a 'camcorder' – combined video camera and recorder.

A **telecine** is a device that converts a film to an electrical video format. When film was used for TV newsgathering, a telecine was then needed to convert from the film to an electrical format for TV broadcast.

A **wideband cable** is a cable capable of conveying a wide bandwidth signal. For digital signals, that would mean a high data rate – lots of bits per second. However, here Taylor is talking about an analogue signal and he means a cable capable of carrying a wide range of frequencies. In both cases – analogue and digital – a wideband cable is the sort of cable needed to carry video signals and high-quality audio. It is in contrast to narrowband, which would be capable only of carrying less demanding signals, such as telephone-quality audio.

As noted earlier, at first satellite communications could be used only for communication between fixed locations on the earth, but with further advances in technology, satellite ground stations could be mobile. Initially they could be mounted on a vehicle, but now they can even be small enough to be carried. Satellites allow communication to remote regions of the Earth where the infrastructure does not exist for any other means of communication (**communications dead spots**, as Taylor refers to them), which allowed for satellite newsgathering (**SNG**). The (satellite) **uplink** is the communication path from the ground to the satellite. The other direction is the **downlink**.

The **IBA** is the Independent Broadcasting Authority. This was the body set up to regulate commercial television and radio. It became the ITC (Independent Television Commission) in 1990, which in turn ceased to exist in December 2003 when its function was taken over by OFCOM, the Office of Communications.

The **Newshawk** is a portable satellite ground station, which can be connected to a video camera, used for satellite newsgathering.

Activity 6 (self-assessment)

What does Taylor say are the disadvantages of film which were overcome by moving to analogue electronic video gathered using the Hawkeye?

Comment

The answer is given at the end of this part.

Into the digital era

Remember that this paper was written in 1995, at which time digital techniques were just beginning to take over in electronic newsgathering. Taylor therefore concludes his paper with comments on the nature and impact of changing to digital techniques.

By the mid-1990s therefore one could be forgiven for thinking that news providers had all the technology they needed to deliver real news from more or less anywhere in the world.

And indeed we have.

So what is it that now attracts news companies to an all digital solution for newsgathering, post production and transmission?

Well, the traditional broadcast industry view is of course well known: digital brings consistent high quality pictures and sound from reliable, stable equipment which requires minimal or in some cases zero routine **alignment.**

Digital techniques together with advances in **VLSI** and [other developments in electronics], have opened the way for **video signal processing** to be carried out on economically priced standard computer platforms, with appropriate software, to give broadcasters much greater choice and ever more function per pound spent – great news when wrestling with hard-pressed capital budgets.

These benefits are attractive to news companies too, but the real bonus which drives our interest is the potential for digital computer based solutions to deliver high quality news programmes free from the **multigeneration limitations** of analogue **VTRs** and the editorial inflexibility of tape based production where **stories cannot easily be altered** or updated <u>and</u> at the same time achieve substantial operational cost savings.

[...]

[L]et me conclude by highlighting what I believe to be the digital newsgathering promise:

- More efficient newsgathering.
- More options for getting the story back.
- Faster **post production.**
- Greater editorial freedom.
- Broad multiskilling opportunities.
- Easier automation.
- Improved technical quality.
- Lower operating costs.

I make no excuse for emphasising the cost saving elements that digital news operations should achieve.

News companies are having to compete in an ever more cost conscious broadcasting industry. Our greatest asset is our staff but regrettably it is also our most expensive cost.

Yes, all the quality and other operational benefits of this technology are highly desirable and contribute toward a news provider's competitive edge, but at the end of the day it is the potential cost savings primarily achieved through multiskilling and job elimination which are the main attraction to news providers.

It is for this reason that I stated at the start of my presentation that the impact of this particular technology revolution is going to be bigger than anything we have experienced in the past.

[...]

Alignment. Analogue electronic equipment often requires adjustments in order for it to perform at its best. On magnetic tapes, for example, it might be necessary to adjust the position of the record and playback heads on the tape, and the record and playback levels might have to be adjusted up or down. Generally speaking, it is much easier to make digital systems independent of alignments. This is because the exact details of the symbol do not matter, provided you can tell whether a symbol is representing a 1 or a 0.

VLSI is very-large-scale integration. Originally, electronic circuits were built from 'discrete components' (such as resistors, capacitors, inductors and transistors – but you do not need to know what these all are). A single component would do one job, and a complicated electronic circuit would be built up from many components. Later, integrated circuits (ICs) came along, which combined many components on a single 'silicon chip'. As the technology advanced, more and more components could be fitted onto a single integrated circuit so that the single device (single chip) could do more and more advanced functions. Integrating large numbers of components onto a single chip was called 'large-scale integration', then getting even more onto a chip was 'very-large-scale integration'. I am not sure if anyone has precisely defined 'large' and 'very large' in this context.

Video signal processing. When you have an image encoded electronically (the video signal), you can manipulate it to do things like change colours or remove unnecessary detail. Manipulating a signal in this way, for whatever purpose, is known as signal processing.

Multigenerational limitations. Each time a copy is made from an analogue signal – video or audio – there is inevitably a degradation in quality, because copying can never be perfect. Thus, there is a limit to the number of 'generations' of copies that can be made. The maximum number of generations before the quality becomes unacceptable depends upon the copying process and the application, but typically we are talking in terms of three or four. With digital signals this effect can be virtually eliminated, because digital signals can be regenerated and then they are 'as good as new'.

VTR stands for video tape recorder.

Stories cannot easily be altered. As I shall be discussing later, the fact that stories can be easily altered with digital systems is not always beneficial!

The term *post production* refers to the collection of processes that are done to a sequence of video or audio after the filming or recording. The processes include editing and signal processing.

Activity 7 (self-assessment)

Taylor's paper highlights a number of important dates in the development of newsgathering and news broadcasts. A good way of getting a picture of historical developments is to plot events on a time line. Figure 2 begins this for some of the events mentioned by Taylor. Go back over Taylor's paper and extract more dates to add to a copy of the time line. (I found another eleven events to add.) Note that the use of '*c*', an abbreviation for 'circa' meaning 'about', indicates an approximate date, as in *c*.1970 for 'about 1970'.

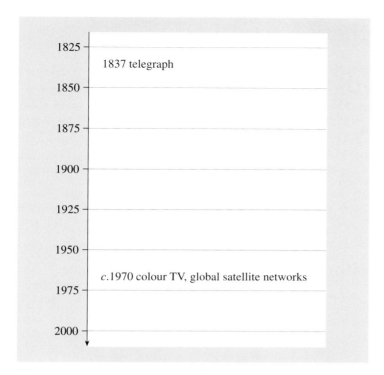

Figure 2   Start of a time line for Activity 7

Comment

My answer is given at the end of this part.

Activity 8 (self-assessment)

· ·

When considering the relationship between technology and society it is often helpful to consider influences in two directions:

1   Technology push. Newly developed technology creates a need that wasn't there before.
2   Demand (or market) pull. Users have a need, and technology is deliberately developed to satisfy that need.

Thinking in terms of the user as the news industry (journalists, and newspaper, radio or TV businesses in general), there is evidence of both technology push and demand pull in Taylor's description.

Identify one example of each, and support your answer with quotes from Taylor's paper.

Comment

My answer is given at the end of this part.

· ·

3 Newsgathering now

Taylor's paper, *From Newsreels To Real News*, provided a historical overview of newsgathering up to the time the paper was written in 1995. It provides a good background but is out of date as I write this in 2005 (ten years is a very long time in the recent history of ICT). Taylor wrote an updating paper for T175, *Real News Meets IT,* and you can find this on the course website. I shall be drawing on *Real News Meets IT* in later sections of this part of Block 3, but you do not need to read it yourself unless you are particularly interested. Instead, in this section I have reproduced an extract from a book (Higgins, 2004) which introduces the principal elements used by a TV station to get a report for broadcast.

3.1   Introduction to SNG and ENG microwave

Higgins says that his book was written to offer 'beginning professionals in satellite and electronic newsgathering an introduction to the technologies and processes involved in covering an event'. Like Taylor, Higgins worked in the news industry for many years and so has the authority of an 'insider'.

The extract here is from the beginning of the book and you should be able to follow most of the content from what you already know. As you read, try to make links with the issues raised in Taylor's paper as well as your developing understanding of ICT generally. I also found it helpful to think about news reports that I have seen on television to set the paper into a context that I could recognise.

Introduction to SNG and ENG Microwave

J. Higgins

2004

Elsevier Focal Press

Basic Overview of the Role of ENG/SNG

Television newsgathering is the process by which materials, i.e. pictures and sound, that help tell a story about a particular event are acquired and sent back to the studio. On arrival, they may be either relayed directly live to the viewer, or edited (packaged) for later transmission.

The process of newsgathering is a complex one, typically involving a cameraman and a reporter, a means of delivering the story back to the studio, and for live coverage, voice communication from the studio back to the reporter at the scene of the story.

Coverage of a sports event involves essentially the same elements but on a much greater scale. Instead of a single reporter you would have a number of commentators, and instead of a single cameraman, you might have up to thirty or forty cameras covering a major international golf tournament.

Whether it is a news or a sports event, the pictures and sound have to be sent back. This could be done by simply recording the coverage onto tape, and then taking it back to the studio. However, because of the need for immediacy, it is far more usual to send the coverage back by using a satellite or terrestrial microwave link, or via a fibre optic connection provided by, say, the telephone company.

[...]

As I shall discuss in Section 5.2, tape is likely to be replaced by other storage media over the next few years. The story described here would be essentially the same, though, using, say, flash memory.

Principal Elements in Covering an Event

Let us just look at the principal elements of covering a news story from where it happens on location to its transmission from the TV studio.

We will pick a type of story that is of local and possibly national interest. Just suppose the story is the shooting of a police officer during a car chase following an armed robbery.

Camera and sound

The shooting happened around 2.30 pm, and the TV station newsroom was tipped off shortly after by a phone call from a member of the public at the scene.

Having checked the truth of the story with the police press office, by 3.00 pm the newsroom at the TV station despatched a cameraman (generically applied to both male and female camera operators) and a reporter to the location.

Generally these days, the cameraman is responsible for both shooting the pictures and recording the sound. The reporter finds out all the information on the circumstances of the armed robbery, the car chase and the shooting of the police officer. The cameraman may be shooting 'GVs' – general views of the scene and its surroundings onto tape – or interviews between the reporter, police spokesmen and eyewitnesses.

The reporter then will typically record a piece-to-camera (PTC) ... which is where the reporter stands at a strategic point against a background which sets the scene for the story – perhaps the location where the officer was shot, the police station, or the hospital where the officer has been taken – and recounts the events, speaking and looking directly into the camera.

So by 5.00 pm the cameraman has several tapes (termed 'rushes'), showing the scene, interviews and the reporter's PTC. Now, will this material be edited on site to present the story, or will the rushes be sent directly back to the station to be edited ready for the studio to use in the 6.00 pm bulletin?

Editing

The 'cutting together' of the pictures and sound to form a 'cut-piece' or 'package' used to be carried out mostly back at the studio.

Mobile edit vehicles were usually only deployed on the 'big stories', or where there was editorial pressure to produce a cut-piece actually in the field. In the latter part of the 1990s, with the increasing use of the compact digital tape formats, the major manufacturers introduced laptop editors.

The laptop editor has both a tape player and a recorder integrated into one unit, with two small TV screens and a control panel. These units, which are slightly larger and heavier than a laptop computer, can be used either by a picture editor, or more commonly nowadays, by the cameraman.

During the 1990s, the pressure on TV organisations to reduce costs led to the introduction of multi-skilling, where technicians, operators and journalists are trained in at least one (and often two) other crafts apart from their primary core skill.

However, the production of a news story is rarely a contiguous serial process – more commonly, several tasks need to be carried out in parallel. For instance, the main package may need to be begun to be edited while the cameraman has to go off and shoot some extra material.

The combination of skills can be quite intriguing, so we can have a cameraman who can record sound and edit tape; a reporter who can also edit tape and/ or shoot video and record sound (often referred to as a video journalist or VJ); or a microwave technician who can operate a camera and edit.

So it is often a juggling act to make sure that the right number of people with the right combination of skills available are on location all at the same time.

Getting the story back

There are now three options as to how we get the story back to the studio for transmission on the 6 o'clock news bulletin – it can be:

- taken back in person by the reporter and/or the cameraman
- sent back via motorbike despatch rider
- transmitted from an ENG microwave or SNG microwave truck.

The first two are obvious and so we need not concern ourselves any further. The third option is of course what we are focused on – and in any case, is the norm nowadays for sending material in this type of situation from location back to the studio.

As it turns out, the newsdesk – realizing the scale of the story once the reporter was on the scene – had despatched a microwave truck down to the location at 4.00 pm. The ENG microwave or SNG truck (for our purposes here it does not matter which) finds a suitable position, and establishes a link back to the studio, with both programme and technical communications in place.

By just gone 5.00 pm, the tape material (rushes or edited package) is replayed from the VTR in the truck back to the studio.

Going live

The reporter may actually have to do a 'live' report back to the studio during the news bulletin, and this is accomplished by connecting the camera to the microwave link truck (along with sound signal from the reporter's microphone) either via a cable, a fibre optic connection or using a short-range microwave link [...].

From the studio, a 'feed' of the studio presenter's microphone is radioed back to the truck, and fed into an earpiece in the reporter's ear, so that the studio presenter can ask the reporter questions about the latest on the situation. The reporter will also be provided with a small picture monitor (out of camera shot) so that they can see an 'off-air' feed of the bulletin.

This is commonly known as a 'live two-way', and what the viewer sees is a presentation of the story, switching between the studio and the location. [...]

Typical transmission chain

We now have all the elements that form the transmission chain between the location and the studio, enabling either taped or live material to be transmitted.

The camera and microphone capture the pictures and sound. The material is then perhaps edited on site, and then the pictures and sound – whether rushes, edited or 'live' – are sent back via the truck (ENG microwave or SNG) to the TV station.

The processes that occur at either end of the chain are the same no matter whether the signals are sent back via terrestrial microwave or via satellite.

[...]

Activity 9 (self-assessment)

Earlier we saw that Taylor suggested eight areas in which digital methods promised improvements:

1   More efficient newsgathering.
2   More options for getting the story back.
3   Faster post production.
4   Greater editorial freedom.
5   Broad multiskilling opportunities.
6   Easier automation.
7   Improved technical quality.
8   Lower operating costs.

Can you see any of these appearing in Higgins's description?

Comment

My answer is given at the end of this part.

3.2   ICT processes in newsgathering

The generic diagram of a communication system, as discussed previously, is shown in Figure 3. If we think of newsgathering as communication from the reporter in the field (User 1) to news editors in the studio (User 2), then we can relate some of the processes described by Higgins to the processes in the boxes. Note in particular Higgins' summary of the 'typical transmission chain':

> The camera and microphone capture the pictures and sound. The material is then perhaps edited on site, and then the pictures and sound – whether rushes, edited or 'live' – are sent back via the truck (ENG microwave or SNG) to the TV station.
>
> Higgins (2004)

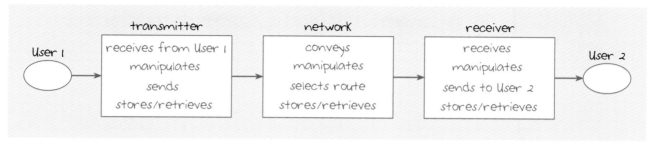

Figure 3 Generic diagram of a communication system

So at the *transmitter* we have:

> Receives from User 1. This is done by the camera and microphone, which convert the image and sound to electrical signals.

> Manipulates. Editing on site is an example of manipulation.

> Send. The transmitter on the truck sends the signals via microwave.

> Stores/retrieves. Higgins describes the material being recorded to tape (remember that the unedited recorded tapes are referred to as 'rushes'), and then retrieved (either the rushes or edited) to send back to the studio.

The only *network* activity described here is 'conveying'. The main focus of Higgins's description involves conveying via microwave, but he also makes reference to taking the story on tapes back in person or using a motorbike despatch rider.

Equipment at the TV studio, including video servers and the computers used by the editors, constitute the *receiver*. Here, the microwave signal (or the tapes) is received, and manipulated if any further editing is required. If the item is not being broadcast live then it will be stored and subsequently retrieved at the time of broadcast – presumably it is in any case stored for archive purposes.

I shall now look in more detail at some of the technology used in the field.

4 Anatomy of a digital camcorder

The development of portable camcorders capable of recording long sequences of high-quality video has been important for newsgathering, but camcorders are also very popular consumer items. In this section I shall be looking in more detail at elements of a camcorder, using it as an example of an ICT system which you are probably familiar with to some extent. Even if you have not used one yourself you will have seen them being used or seen them in shops. (If you get the opportunity, you may like to have a look at a modern digital camcorder in a high-street shop.)

'Camcorder' is a contraction of '(video) **cam**era and re**corder**'. There is an implication in this context that a video camera alone might not record (store) the image. Whereas a film camera always stores an image (on film), a video camera might only convert the image to an electrical signal for display remotely on a TV monitor. For example, you can buy video cameras for domestic security which allow you to view outside your house by displaying the output of a camera on your television. If you connect one of these cameras to a video recorder you can record what you see, but the video camera does not itself contain storage. A camcorder is a combination of the two: the camera which converts the image to an electrical signal and a video recorder which records the electrical signal.

Figure 4 represents a camcorder based on the model introduced earlier in the course.

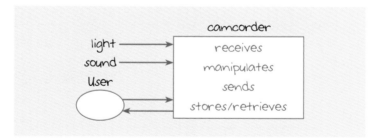

Figure 4   Model of camcorder

Activity 10 (exploratory)

How does Figure 4 differ from the model of a stand-alone computer that you have seen before?

Comment

The only difference in the diagram is that the model of the camcorder has light and sound as additional inputs.

You would not normally think of a camcorder as a computer, but for our purposes, in the context of ICT, this is a useful starting point. A camcorder does indeed contain a computer which, because it is hidden from the user and it takes inputs from other sources as well as the user, is called an **embedded computer** . In Figure 4 we draw attention to this feature of the camcorder – the embedded computer – neglecting other features that are for the present purposes irrelevant. Nothing about the shape, the construction materials or the power source appear on Figure 4, for example, although these are all important in other contexts. Also, Figure 4 does not include any details of the things that it shows.

embedded computer

The approach to understanding a device or system by focusing on particular aspects and neglecting details is a common tool of technology, and is known as **abstraction** . Typically, to analyse a device or system you start at a high level of abstraction, where you consider only very broad features, then move to a lower level of abstraction where you look at more details. This is what I shall do for the camcorder, and in the next section I look at some of the processes involved in receiving light and sound.

abstraction

4.1   Sound and light input

Figure 5 shows a model of a camcorder at a lower level of abstraction than Figure 4, concentrating on the input of light and sound.

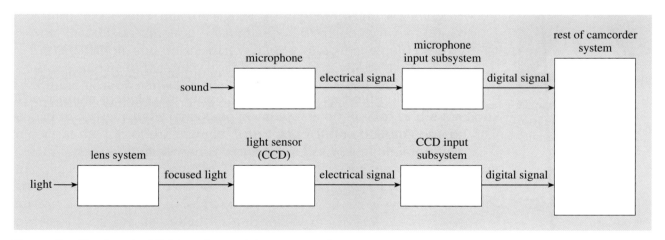

Figure 5   The input of light and sound to a camcorder

Activity 11 (exploratory)

Although Figure 5 shows more details of the light and sound input than Figure 4, some other aspects of the camcorder are shown in less detail than in Figure 4. What things have gone, and can you suggest why I haven't shown them?

Comment

In Figure 5 I have not shown the list of processes – receives, sends, stores/retrieves, manipulates – nor have I shown the oval labelled 'user' with the two input/output arrows. I have omitted these things because I am concerned specifically with the light and sound inputs, and the other features would be a distraction for the moment. This is an important feature of abstraction: selecting what is important.

I shall now go on to discuss the components shown in Figure 5 in more detail.

Microphone

A microphone converts sound in the air to an electrical signal.

Activity 12 (self-assessment)

From what you learnt earlier in the course, what is the name used for a device that converts energy or information from one medium to another?

Comment

The answer is given at the end of this part.

As you have seen before, sounds consists of pressure waves in (usually) the air, and to reproduce a particular sound it is necessary to reproduce the corresponding pattern of pressure waves. A microphone converts the pressure waves in the air to the same pattern of voltage waves on a wire. If this pattern of voltage variation is applied to a loudspeaker, the speaker converts the electrical signal back to pressure waves in the air, reproducing the sound.

Microphone input subsystem

We'll now move on to consider the microphone input subsystem.

Activity 13 (exploratory)

Is the output from the microphone an analogue or a digital signal?

Comment

The output from a microphone is an analogue electrical signal. Just as sound in the air involves continuous pressure variations over a continuous range, so the voltage from the microphone varies continuously over a continuous range.

Because I am considering here a digital camcorder, the analogue audio signal will be converted to a digital signal, and this is the main

function of the microphone input subsystem. The digital audio signal might also be compressed, and put into a standard format.

Lens system

The function of the lens system is to project an image onto the CCD light sensor. A well-designed system ensures that the image is sharp – in focus – and bright. To achieve this, what is needed is a good-quality glass lens (or rather a series of lenses) and accurate focusing. The brightness of the image depends upon the size of the lens. The bigger the lens, the brighter the image, but bigger lenses are more difficult to make and therefore more expensive. Also, of course, bigger lenses mean bigger and heavier cameras. As so often in technology there are trade-offs between several factors. In this case, brightness of the image (and therefore the ability of the camera to operate in low light levels) interacts with cost, size, weight and image quality. I shall discuss focusing in more detail later, after describing the light sensor.

CCD light sensor

The **CCD light sensor** is a transducer that converts light to an electrical signal. CCD stands for 'charge coupled device', and physically a CCD light sensor is an integrated circuit with a transparent cover. A photograph of one is shown in Figure 6. Under the cover is a rectangular array of light-sensitive electronic components called photosites. You do not need to know the mechanism involved, but each photosite provides an analogue electrical output that measures how bright the light is on that site. Each photosite can therefore contribute one pixel to the detected image. Important parameters of a CCD light sensor are the size of the light-sensitive area and the number of photosites – and hence the number of pixels in the image it can produce.

CCD light sensor

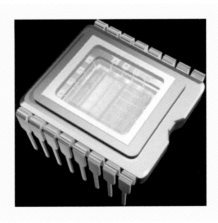

Figure 6 Picture of a CCD (source: www.nanoelectronics.jp)

The size of the device is usually expressed in terms of the length of a diagonal line from one corner of the rectangle to the other. As you often

find in ICT, advances in the technology lead to a reduction in the size, with the same or better performance and maybe lower cost. CCD sensors are an example of this as Taylor observes in his 2004 updating paper:

> [There has been] the widespread adoption of small hand held mini-camcorders producing good quality images from small 1/3rd inch CCDs originally developed for the consumer market. An enormous amount of Japanese development effort has gone into producing high resolution, high sensitivity small CCDs to the point where a current 1/3rd inch CCD produces better all round performance than a standard 2/3rd inch broadcast format camcorder of 5 years ago, but at around only 20% of the cost. Now there is a trend to move to 1/5th inch CCDs which will enable even cheaper and more compact camcorders. This lower cost has enabled news companies to put greater numbers of camcorders into the field and gather a wider cross section of material.
>
> Taylor (2004)

For high-resolution images large numbers of pixels are needed, and at the time of writing, camcorders can have up to several 'megapixels', where one megapixel is 1 000 000 pixels (10^6 pixels).

Activity 14 (self-assessment)

If a camcorder has a CCD with an array of 811 pixels horizontally by 508 pixels vertically, how many pixels is that in total? Give your answer to two significant figures using scientific notation.

Comment

The answer is given at the end of this part.

The output from one photosite on a CCD is a measure of how bright the light is at that site. It contains no information about the colour of the light. To get colour information, coloured filters are placed in front of the CCD so that separate photosites measure the brightness in each of the three primary colours of light: red, blue and green.

Some cameras use separate CCDs for each of the three colours whereas others use a single CCD with different coloured filters interleaved over individual sites, but the details of the configuration of the filters does not concern us here. If you want to know more you will be able to find information by searching on the Web.

Instead of using CCDs for light sensors, some cameras use CMOS (complementary metal oxide semiconductor) sensors. There are differences between CCD sensors and CMOS sensors – broadly speaking CCD sensors provide better image quality but cameras using CMOS sensors can be smaller – but at the level of the discussion here they essentially perform the same function.

I shall now return to the lens system of the camera, to explain how it focuses the light.

Focusing

Focusing is done by adjusting the size of the gap between the lens and the light sensor. To get distant objects in focus, the gap needs to be smaller than that required for close objects (see Figure 7).

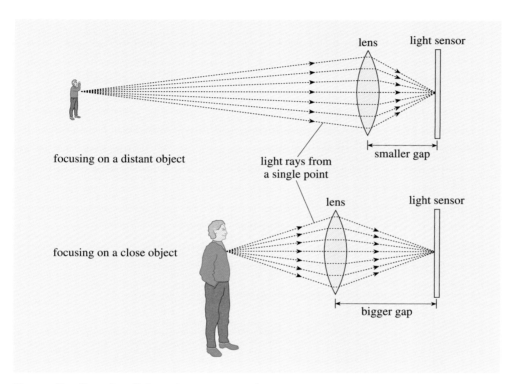

Figure 7   Focusing light using a camera lens

In theory the exact gap size is determined by the exact distance to the object being filmed. In practice, one gap size will be adequate for a range of object distances, this range being called the 'depth of field'.

Focusing in a camcorder is invariably done with an electric motor moving a lens, and there will be a facility to focus automatically (autofocus). Auto focusing is either passive or active.

Passive autofocusing works by a computer embedded in the camera examining the image (from the light sensor) to determine whether it is in focus or not.

Activity 15 (exploratory)

How do you decide whether an image is in focus? What do you think the camera's computer can look for to determine whether the image is in focus?

Comment

You can tell whether an image is in focus by seeing how 'sharp' it is. The camera's computer looks for sharp edges – sudden changes in colour or brightness. These abrupt changes will be present only if the image is in focus.

Under control of the camera's computer, the motor will move the lens in and out to find the best focus, identified by the presence of sharp lines in the image.

Active autofocusing works by the camera measuring the distance to the object viewed, and using that to calculate the gap needed between lens and light sensor. It measures the distance by sending out pulses of infrared light towards the object being filmed, and measuring how long it takes the reflected light to get back to the camera. During this time, between sending the pulse and detecting the reflected pulse, the light does a round trip – it travels out and back again. The time the light takes to go one way is therefore half the measured interval. I'll call this time – half the time between sending and receiving the pulse – the transit time.

The speed of light is known, so the transit time can be used to calculate the distance between the camera and the object.

Specifically, the distance from the camera to the object is given by the transit time multiplied by the speed of light.

distance to the object = transit time × speed of light

This can be written much more concisely using

d for the distance to the object

t for the transit time

c for the speed of light.

Then I can write:

$$d = t \times c$$

When writing equations like this, it is a convention that you can miss out the multiplication symbol. Any numbers or letters written next to each other are taken to be multiplied together, so we can write:

$$d = t\,c$$

Equations relating three quantities in this particular way, where one (in this case d) is given by multiplying the other two (in this case t and c) together, are quite common, and you will be meeting other examples later in this part of Block 3. For reasons which will become clearer later, it is useful to draw this type of equation in a 'formula triangle', as shown in Figure 8. The quantities that are multiplied together go in the bottom two corners (it doesn't matter which way around), and the thing they

Strictly, c is the speed of light in free space (a vacuum). In the atmosphere – through air – light travels at almost the same speed as in a vacuum, and we can neglect the difference. In glass, however, light travels substantially slower (about two-thirds the speed) and it is necessary to take account of this fact when considering light in optical fibre.

calculate goes in the top corner. I am not going to say anything more about the formula triangle for the moment, though it might be a bit mysterious, but it will become clearer later.

I now want to put in a value for the speed of light, c, so that I will have a formula that allows me to calculate the distance d directly from the transit time t.

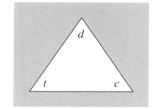

Figure 8   A formula triangle

The speed of light in metres per second is 3×10^8. That is to say, light travels $3 \times 10^8 = 300\ 000\ 000$ metres every second. When I am doing calculations related to the focusing of the camera, however, I will find the times I am using will be much smaller than a second and the relevant distances will usually be of the order of a few metres – not three hundred million metres! What I am going to do, therefore, is express the speed of light in terms of how far it travels in one nanosecond (ns), which is one thousand-millionth of a second:

$$1\ \text{ns} = \frac{1}{1\ 000\ 000\ 000}\ \text{s} = \frac{1}{10^9}\ \text{s}$$

Activity 16 (exploratory)

How far will light travel in one nanosecond?

Comment

Light travels 300 000 000 metres in one second, so in one nanosecond it travels:

$$\frac{300\ 000\ 000}{1\ 000\ 000\ 000} = 0.3\ \text{metres}$$

So I can express the speed of light as 0.3 m/ns (0.3 metres per nanosecond). But this means that when I write the equation, t represents a time in nanoseconds and d represents a distance in metres. It is important that all the units match. Using a value of $c = 0.3$ m/ns and provided t and d are in nanoseconds and metres respectively, I get:

$$d = t\ 0.3$$

It doesn't matter which way round you write a multiplication (4×5 is the same as 5×4) and it is a convention always to put numbers before letters, so this would normally be written:

$$d = 0.3\ t$$

For example, if the transit time is 20 ns, the distance in metres is given by:

$$d = 0.3\ t = 0.3 \times 20 = 6$$

So the distance is 6 m.

Activity 17 (self-assessment)

. . . .

If the transit time is 14 ns, how far away is the object?

Comment

The answer is given at the end of this part.

Algebra and the use of symbols

The use of symbols to represent numerical values, such as '*d*' for distance, '*t*' for time, '*c*' for the speed of light, is the starting point for algebra. If you don't like maths this might be worrying, but I hope that when you get used to it – and simple familiarity goes a long way to demystifying algebra – you will see that at least it provides useful shorthand.

If you know that *c* is being used to represent the value for the speed of light and *t* a time duration, then you will automatically read $c \times t$ as 'multiply the speed of light by the time duration'. It is helped – when you are used to it – by the fact that the speed of light is nearly always represented by *c*, and that *t* refers to time in lots of different contexts. Notice, incidentally, that there is a subtle difference in the use of *c* compared with *d* and *t*, because *c* is a fixed number, but *d* and *t* can change. We say that *c* is a 'constant' whereas *d* and *t* are 'variables'.

Besides the use of symbols being a shorthand, there is much that you can do by 'manipulating' them, but you will only be meeting this at a simple level in T175. There is more about algebra in *The Sciences Good Study Guide,* Maths Help, Section 9 (Northedge et al., 1997).

Remember that the reason for discussing this calculation was to show that when using active focusing the camcorder can measure the distance to an object by transmitting and detecting an infrared pulse. Active autofocusing therefore involves another output from and input to the camcorder (sending and receiving the infrared pulse). We can show this by adding it to the high-level diagram of a camcorder that was shown in Figure 4, to get that shown in Figure 9.

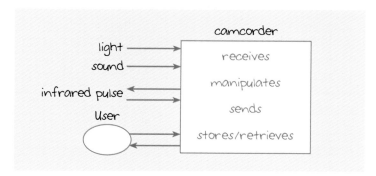

Figure 9 Model of camcorder with active autofocusing

At a lower level of abstraction, the components of the active autofocusing are shown in Figure 10, together with other relevant components of the camcorder.

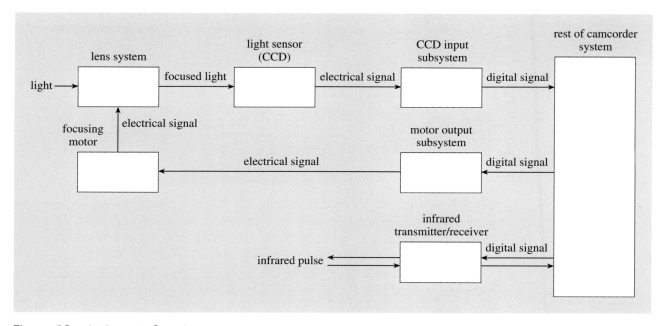

Figure 10 Active autofocusing

Figure 10 is similar to Figure 5, but I have removed the detail of the sound subsystem in order to concentrate on the light and focusing subsystems.

Activity 18 (exploratory)

Write down what you think is done by each of the following boxes in Figure 10.

1   Infrared transmitter/receiver

2   Motor output subsystem

3   Focusing motor.

Comment

1   The infrared transmitter/receiver receives a digital signal from the rest of the camcorder which instructs it to generate and transmit a pulse of infrared light. It also detects the reflected pulse of infrared light which it reports back to the rest of the camcorder in the form of a digital signal.

2   The motor output subsystem receives a digital signal from the rest of the camcorder which it converts to the appropriate analogue electrical signal that drives the focusing motor.

3   The focusing motor changes the position of the lenses so that light is focused in the light sensor. It is controlled by the electrical signal it receives from the motor output subsystem.

4.2   Recorder

The descriptions of newsgathering in the extracts by Taylor and Higgins make reference to videotapes because, until recently, tape was the main storage medium used for video. Camcorders had a built-in VTR (videotape recorder) and in the first camcorders the video was recorded as an analogue signal. Camcorders used for ENG (electronic news gathering) now store the video as a digital signal, whatever medium is used for recording. Camcorders are now appearing which can store the digital video on DVDs or on memory cards.

Taylor (2004) compares DVD-based camcorders and memory-card camcorders in his updating paper; an extract from this follows.

[...]

[T]wo quite different solutions are competing for the TV news broadcaster's camcorder business:

• DVD based camcorders

• Solid state flash memory based camcorders

Ever since the development of the DVD, its potential as a rugged, compact, random access medium has made it attractive to TV news companies as an alternative to video tape for use in camcorders and also as an archive medium. It is not surprising therefore that at least one broadcast equipment manufacturer (Sony) is currently introducing camcorders and field players using the latest 'blue disk' DVD technology [...] which offers approximately 27 GB recording capacity on a 120 mm disk. At 25 Mbps this provides about two and a half hours of recording. The hope is that the blue disks will soon be compatible with the DVD drives available in standard laptops thus facilitating convenient low cost field editing.

There are a few physical limitations with this solution due to the size of the disk, its susceptibility to vibration and unreliability of the disk burning process at low temperatures. However, careful design is minimising the impact of these limitations and a number of TV news organisations are changing over to DVD acquisition.

Even more exciting, last year [2003] Panasonic showed a prototype completely solid state camcorder (called P2 CAM) using four of the consumer SD [secure data] flash memory cards embedded in a standard PCMCIA package called the P2 card. Using 1 GB SD cards each P2 card supplies an initial 4 GB memory capacity. The camcorder holds five P2 cards to give it a total recording duration at 25 Mbps video of about 90 minutes (allowing for audio channels and overheads). Clearly this camcorder totally overcomes the physical limitations which are inevitable with any mechanical recording system and it created enormous interest from the broadcast industry. It is now in production and being evaluated by a number of TV news companies.

PCMCIA : Personal Computer Memory Card International Association, an industry trade association that creates standards for the memory cards that slot into notebook computers and other small portable devices.

The convenience of simply taking the P2 card out of the camcorder and slotting it directly into a laptop computer for editing and downloading to the station server system, via the Internet if necessary, was instantly appreciated. The Achilles' heel of this otherwise ideal solution is the cost of the SD media, but as experience indicates, the cost per Gigabyte of flash memory is reducing by a factor of around 4 per annum. It will not be too long before individual SD cards reach 16 GB capacity at affordable prices. Each P2 card would then be capable of storing nearly five hours at 25 Mbps – more than enough capacity to handle HD

[high definition] TV at 100 Mbps! It is also worth noting that Panasonic point out that, unlike tape, the SD cards are 'non-consumables' lasting the life of the camera. Therefore only a relatively small number of cards are required for each camera as the content should be downloaded into station servers soon after shooting, thus freeing up the cards and making the cost of the medium unimportant.

When either, or both, of these new acquisition technologies replace video tape based camcorders over the next couple of years the migration of the TV news industry to IT technology will be complete. It will have been an extraordinary revolution in terms of its implementation speed having taken less than 10 years from servers and hard disk editing systems first attracting TV news companies' attention. Remarkably it is only around 25 years since Electronic News Gathering ousted film and ushered in the all electronic era.

Taylor (2004)

Tape, DVD and memory cards use three different physical principles for storing data (Figure 11), and have different merits and limitations.

Figure 11 Storage media

Tape is a magnetic storage medium. In very general terms, data is stored by the orientation of the magnetic field in microscopic particles on the tape. The orientation is set when writing to the tape and detected when reading from it. Tape is cheap and can store large amounts of data, but has the significant disadvantage that it can only be written to and read

from sequentially. It is not possible to jump to somewhere in the middle of the tape; you have to run through it to get there. Also, compared with DVDs and memory cards, tape is less robust. It can be quite easily damaged and wears out after repeated use.

As you learned earlier in the course, a DVD is an optical storage medium. Data is written to it by putting microscopic marks on the surface of the disk. Data is read from it by detecting the presence of the marks, which is done by shining a laser onto the surface and measuring the amount of light reflected. Depending on the type of disk, writing to the disk may be permanent or reversible (for a DVD-RW, rewritable, disk). DVDs are now cheap and robust. Certainly data can be read from the disk any number of times with no significant degradation to the disk, and RW disks can be rewritten many times. DVDs do not need to be read serially like tape because it is possible to jump straight to anywhere on the disk – they are **random access**.

random access

Memory cards use flash memory, which is an electrical storage medium, used in an increasing range of applications including digital (still) cameras. Microscopic cells in an integrated circuit can be set to a voltage and they remain at that voltage by holding electrical charge even when the power is disconnected, until deliberately changed. Some types of flash memory are random access, but others require sequential access. Writing to and reading from memory cards is faster than with a DVD.

Whereas a tape has to be moved physically through a VTR, and a DVD is spun around as the read/write 'head' moves across the disk, there are no moving parts involved in using a memory card. This is what Taylor is referring to when he says they are **solid state**. Generally speaking, moving parts are more prone to wear and tear and failure, so solid state components tend to be more reliable and last for longer. The equipment for reading and writing to flash memory is therefore more rugged than that for tapes and DVDs.

solid state

There is an associated computer (spreadsheet) activity in Part 3, Section 3.4, which models the falling cost of flash memory. You can do this now, or wait until a more convenient time.

Activity 19 (self-assessment)

Using information from the above discussion, answer the following questions about tape, DVDs and flash memory.

(a) Which allow random access when reading?

(b) Which is solid state?

Comment

The answer is given at the end of this part.

Taylor makes extensive use of approximate calculations on memory sizes, data rates and recording durations in the extract. It is instructive to 'unpick' some of his calculations.

Taylor says that the 27 GB (gigabyte) capacity of the blue disk DVD provides about 2 and a half hours of recording at 25 Mbps (mega bits per second). A gigabyte is about 1 074 000 000 bytes and there are eight bits in a byte, so 27 GB is about:

$$27 \times 1\,074\,000\,000 \times 8 = 232\,000\,000\,000 \text{ bits} = 2.32 \times 10^{11} \text{ bits}$$

(to three significant figures).

At 25 Mbps this is enough storage for:

$$\frac{232\,000\,000\,000}{25\,000\,000} = 9280 \text{ s}$$

Dividing by 60 for the number of seconds in a minute gives 155 minutes, which is indeed 'about two and a half hours'.

About the P2 cards Taylor says:

> four of the consumer SD [secure data] flash memory cards [are] embedded in a standard PCMCIA package called the P2 card. Using 1 GB SD cards each P2 card supplies an initial 4 GB memory capacity.
>
> Taylor (2004)

This is simply saying: $4 \times 1 \text{ GB} = 4 \text{ GB}$.

Taylor then says:

> The camcorder holds five P2 cards to give it a total recording duration at 25 Mbps video of about 90 minutes (allowing for audio channels and overheads).
>
> Taylor (2004)

Five P2 cards will store $5 \times 4 \text{ GB} = 20 \text{ GB}$. That is 20 gigabytes which, using a similar calculation to the one we did above, is about 1.72×10^{11} bits. At 25 Mbps that is enough for:

$$\frac{172\,000\,000\,000}{25\,000\,000} \text{ s} = 6880 \text{ s}$$

Dividing by 60 for the number of seconds in a minute gives about 115 minutes. That is rather more than the 90 minutes that Taylor estimates,

One gigabyte is actually $2^{30} = 1\,073\,741\,824$ bytes, but I don't need all the figures because I only want the answer to three significant figures.

but we have not taken account of the audio coding or any overheads. (Overheads are extra bits that are needed to manage the data – file names, bits to keep the video and audio synchronised, etc.) We don't have any information on how much should be allowed for these other factors, but it seems reasonable that they could account for the difference.

Later, Taylor says:

> It will not be too long before individual SD cards reach 16 GB capacity at affordable prices. Each P2 card would then be capable of storing nearly five hours at 25 Mbps – more than enough capacity to handle HD TV at 100 Mbps!
>
> Taylor (2004)

If an SD card stores 16 GB, then a P2 card (which holds four SD cards) can store 4×16 GB = 64 GB. Using Taylor's claim that 20 GB is enough for about 90 minutes, 64 GB should be enough for about:

$$\frac{64}{20} \times 90 \text{ minutes} = 288 \text{ minutes}$$

Dividing by 60 for the number of minutes in an hour, that is 4.8 hours, which is 'nearly five hours', as Taylor says.

Activity 20 (self-assessment)

Based on Taylor's statement:

> Each P2 card would then be capable of storing nearly five hours at 25 Mbps – more than enough capacity to handle HD TV at 100 Mbps!
>
> Taylor (2004)

approximately what duration of HD TV should a P2 card be capable of storing?

Comment

The answer is given at the end of this part.

4.3   Batteries

Though batteries are in some ways less glamorous than other components of ICT systems, advances in battery technology are every bit as important to the success of ICT as developments in other areas.

Before I can say anything useful about batteries, however, you need to know some basic ideas about electricity.

Voltage, current and resistance

voltage

Voltage (or, more correctly, electromotive force, emf – but I shall follow common practice and just say voltage) – is a measure of the force with which electricity is 'pushed'. Nothing happens, however, unless there is an electric circuit, which is a path from one terminal of a voltage source (the battery, in this case) to the other, along which the electricity can flow (Figure 12).

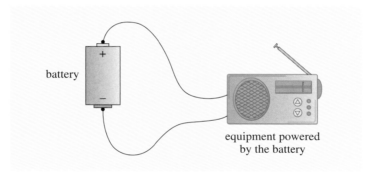

Figure 12   An electric circuit

If there is an electric circuit, the rate at which electricity flows is determined by the nature of the circuit and the value of the battery's voltage. To quantify the rate at which electricity flows we need to know how much the circuit allows or resists the flow of electricity, and this is
resistance
determined by a measure known as **resistance**.

If a circuit has a high resistance, little electricity flows for a given voltage. If it has a low resistance, a lot of electricity flows. Resistance is measured in units called ohms, and the rate of flow of electricity is measured in units called amps. The rate of electricity flow, which we call the electric
current
current, in amps is calculated by dividing the battery voltage in volts by the circuit resistance in ohms.

That is:

$$\text{Current in amps} = \frac{\text{voltage in volts}}{\text{resistance in ohms}}$$

Qualitatively, you might be able to see that this is plausible. The bigger the voltage (the stronger the push), the more current will flow. The bigger the resistance, on the other hand, the smaller the current.

The convention is to use symbols, i for current, v for voltage and r for resistance, so we write:

$$i = \frac{v}{r}$$

For example, if a battery voltage is 3 volts and the circuit resistance is 10 ohms the current flowing is:

$$i = \frac{v}{r} = \frac{3}{10} \text{amps} = 0.3 \text{ amps}$$

The symbol for amps is a capital A, so this is written as 0.3 A. The symbol for volts is a capital V and for ohms is the capital Greek letter omega, Ω.

One amp is a fairly large current flow for electronic equipment, and quite often it is easier to work in units of 1/1000 of an amp which is 1 milliamp, written as 1 mA. Similarly, a resistance of 1 ohm is very small for electronic equipment and often resistance will be expressed in units of kilohms, kΩ, which are thousands of ohms.

Activity 21 (self-assessment)

If the battery voltage is 1 V and the circuit resistance 1 kΩ, what is the current flow in mA?

Comment

The answer is given at the end of this part.

The formula triangle that I introduced earlier can be used with the equation for v, i, and r. This time because v is on the top of the fraction, v goes at the top of the triangle, with i and r in the bottom corners (again it does not matter which way around), resulting in a formula triangle as shown in Figure 13. The relationship between voltage, current and resistance represented by this triangle has a special name: it is known as **Ohm's law**. (Georg Simon Ohm, 1789–1854, was the German physicist who first described this relationship.)

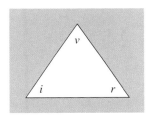

Figure 13 The formula triangle for Ohm's law

Ohm's law

Battery parameters
Now that we have covered some background on electricity, I will return to discussing batteries.

Activity 22 (exploratory)

What do you think would be the important characteristics of a battery for a portable ICT device such as a camcorder or a mobile telephone?

Comment

The things that I thought of as the most important were:

- Weight: if the device is to be portable it must not be too heavy

- Size: for a portable device it needs to be kept small

- Running time: the user does not want to have to replace or recharge the battery too frequently

- Cost: it should not be too expensive.

I'd like to explore how these parameters are specified in more detail. To make the discussion more concrete I'll compare examples of some of the most widely available types of rechargeable battery. I shall look at two different sizes: AA and C. You are probably familiar with these sizes because AA is widely used in portable radios and CD players while the larger C size is used for torches, bicycle lights and portable stereos, among other things. Batteries described as LR6 and MN1500 are the same size as AAs, while R14 and MN1400 are the same size as Cs.

For each of the sizes I shall compare two battery technologies: nickel–cadmium (abbreviated to the chemical symbols NiCd, or called 'NiCad') and nickel–metal hydride (abbreviated to NiMH). At the time of writing, although both NiCd and NiMH batteries are widely available, NiCd batteries are declining rapidly in popularity. I shall have more to say about why this is later, but for the moment it is convenient for my purposes to compare the two technologies.

Batteries produce electricity by a chemical reaction, and nickel–cadmium or nickel–metal hydride refer to the chemicals used in the battery. All NiCd batteries will have some similar characteristics because they use the same chemistry, but different sizes and physical constructions will lead to some differences. Likewise for all NiMH batteries, or any other chemistry.

Some basic data on specific examples of each of these four batteries is given in Table 1.

Table 1   Data based on Ansmann batteries

Size	Chemistry	Voltage	Dimensions		Weight	Capacity	Price
			Height	**Diameter**			
AA	NiCd	1.2 V	50 mm	15 mm	24 g	0.8 Ah	£1.40
AA	NiMH	1.2 V	50 mm	15 mm	24 g	2.1 Ah	£2.50
C	NiCd	1.2 V	60 mm	26 mm	75 g	1.7 Ah	£4.00
C	NiMH	1.2 V	60 mm	26 mm	80 g	3.5 Ah	£7.00

Ah: amp-hours.

Source: Battery Force (http://www.battery-force.co.uk/ [accessed 5 February 2005])

All four batteries in Table 1 provide 1.2 volts. This is a consequence of the chemistry used, and the fact that each one is a single 'cell'. The cell is the basic building block of the battery, and to get higher voltages, cells can be connected together, as shown in Figure 14. This way of connecting cells or batteries, with the positive terminal of one connected to the negative terminal of the next, is know as connecting in series, and results in an output voltage that is the sum of the voltages of the individual batteries. The voltages just add together. You might be familiar with this way of connecting batteries from when you have put batteries in radios or torches, where they are nearly always connected in series.

Strictly the term 'battery' should only be used when there is a combination of cells used together, not for the single cells of an AA or C 'battery', but this is a distinction that is rarely adhered to.

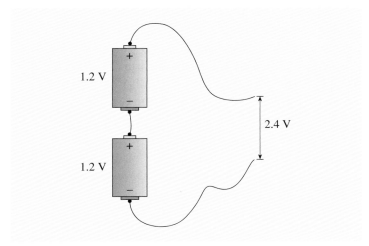

Figure 14 Cells connected together to get a higher voltage

Batteries using a different chemistry produce different voltages from a single cell. A single cell of an alkaline battery (the technology used for the most common non-rechargable batteries) for example, produces 1.5 volts. The chemistry of NiCd and NiMH is similar, so they produce the same voltage as each other.

The battery size, AA or C, characterises the dimensions, expressed as the battery height and diameter.

You can see that the weights of the two AA batteries are the same, and there is only a small difference between the weights of the two C batteries. In fact it is only when we come to the battery capacity and the prices that there is a significant difference between the NiCd and the NiMH batteries.

The NiMH batteries are more expensive but have a greater capacity. The units of capacity, Ah, are 'amp-hours', amps multiplied by hours. The idea behind this is that you can't specify a single value for the length of time a battery can be used because it depends upon the current being drawn from it. If you draw a lower current the battery will last longer. However if you multiply the value of the current being drawn by the length of time it can be used, you get a constant value: the battery capacity.

For example, a battery with a capacity of 1 Ah could supply 1 A for 1 hour, or else it could supply 2 A for half an hour or 0.5 A for 2 hours. More generally, if a battery can run at a current i for t hours, then its capacity is:

$$\text{capacity} = i \times t$$

If you know the capacity of a battery and want to know how long it can be used to supply a given current, then you divide the capacity by the current.

The time for which the battery can be used, t, is given by:

$$t = \frac{\text{capacity}}{i}$$

Activity 23 (self-assessment)

The form of these equations should be starting to be familiar by now. Again, the relationship between capacity, running time (t) and current (i) can be represented by a formula triangle. Draw one now.

Comment

The answer is given at the end of this part.

Activity 24 (self-assessment)

In a test, it is found that a battery can be used for 10 hours supplying a current of 0.4 A.

(a) What is the capacity of the battery in Ah?

(b) If a current of 0.3 A is flowing from the battery, how long can it be used for?

Comment

The answer is given at the end of this part.

It is important to appreciate that the figures quoted for capacity and the length of time a battery can be used depend very strongly on the way it is being used and the temperature. Also, a battery does not just suddenly run out of electricity – it is not like a car running out of petrol where suddenly there is no more and it stops. Rather, while a battery is being used the voltage falls and as the battery runs out (goes 'flat') its voltage drops more quickly. When specifying a battery's capacity a lower limit to the acceptable voltage is specified, and the battery is defined as flat when that lower limit is reached.

Bearing all this in mind, the values for battery capacity are nevertheless useful for comparisons and estimates of battery performance.

Activity 25 (self-assessment)

How long could a device which uses 0.1 A be run from each of the four batteries in Table 1?

Comment

The answer is given at the end of this part.

As you can see from Table 1, for the batteries considered here, a NiMH battery has a greater capacity than a NiCd battery of the same size and weight, but costs more. This is generally true for NiMH compared with NiCd batteries, although as NiMH become more widely used their prices are getting lower. These are not the only considerations when choosing batteries. For example, with rechargeable batteries such as these there are also issues as to how easy they are to recharge and how many times they can be recharged. On these considerations, broadly speaking NiMH batteries come out better than NiCd batteries. Another significant consideration is the fact that cadmium is highly toxic (poisonous) and so NiCd batteries should be handled carefully and should not be disposed of with other waste, but should be recycled so that the cadmium is extracted safely. For all these reasons, NiCd batteries are falling out of favour.

Activity 26 (exploratory)

Have a look for any batteries that you have, especially rechargeable batteries, and see if they say what voltage they are and what capacity they have. Compare them with those in Table 1. Alternatively, if you don't have any rechargable batteries, you can look for adverts to see what information you can find. (Non-rechargeable batteries don't generally quote their capacity.)

Comment

I had an AA NiCd battery. It was labelled as '1.2 V, 0.65 Ah'. This is a lower capacity than the AA NiCd in Table 1. I weighed it in the kitchen scales (on a piece of paper as a precaution, remembering the toxicity of cadmium) and found it was about 55 g. Clearly mine is inferior to some NiCds – heavier and lower capacity – but I don't recall how much it cost (I bought it several years ago).

I also found both NiCds and NiMH batteries advertised in catalogues that I had at home. The catalogue listed NiCd and NiMH batteries with similar capacity to those in Table 1. Some of them quoted the capacity

in mAh, which is milliamp-hours. The value in mAh needs to be divided by 1000 to get Ah so, for example, the capacity of a battery advertised as a 'super high capacity' NiMH AA battery was given as 2300 mAh. This is equal to 2.3 Ah.

Another important type of battery is based on chemical reactions involving lithium. 'Lithium Ion' (Li-ion) batteries are commonly used in laptop computers and other portable ICT equipment.

A complication when comparing Li-ion batteries with NiCd and NiMH batteries is that the voltage delivered by a Li-ion cell is around 3.6 volts, compared with the 1.2 volts of NiCd and NiMH cells. To make fair comparisons of capacity you need to be looking at supplies at the same voltage.

Activity 27 (self-assessment)

If some equipment requires a 3.6 volt power supply it can use a single Li-ion cell. How many NiCd or NiMH cells would it need, and how should they be connected?

Comment

The answer is at the end of this part.

When the different voltages have been taken into account, the capacities of battery packs using Li-ion batteries are greater than packs using NiCd and NiMH batteries for a given size and weight.

There are other pros and cons to Li-ion batteries, and a particular disadvantage is the need to control more carefully the charging and discharging of the batteries, both to maximise the battery life and for safety reasons.

5 Signal transmission

In the discussions of newsgathering in the Taylor and Higgins papers, you saw the significance of the development of systems that allowed long-distance transmission of electronic signals. Initially transmission used metallic wires (remember Taylor's reference to the importance of the 'lines infrastructure' and his mention of the 'wire picture') and later wireless transmission (terrestrial and satellite microwave) became important. In this section I shall look at some aspects of the transmission of digital signals, starting with a close look at the transmission of electrical signals on wires.

5.1   Transmission of electrical signals on wires

Using a wire to transmit a signal is simple in principle: you operate a switch at one place and observe the effect somewhere else. In Figure 15 I have shown this as a light coming on at a remote location. Notice in this diagram the standard symbol for a battery consisting of two parallel lines, one shorter than the other, and the symbol for a light bulb which is a circle with a cross in it. The standard symbol for a switch that can be 'open' or 'closed' consists of two dots and a line which either connects the dots (when the switch is closed as in Figure 15b) or misses one of the dots (when the switch is open, as in Figure 15a). To switch the light on you close the switch so that there is an electric circuit from the battery to the light bulb and back again. To switch the light off you open the switch to 'break' the circuit.

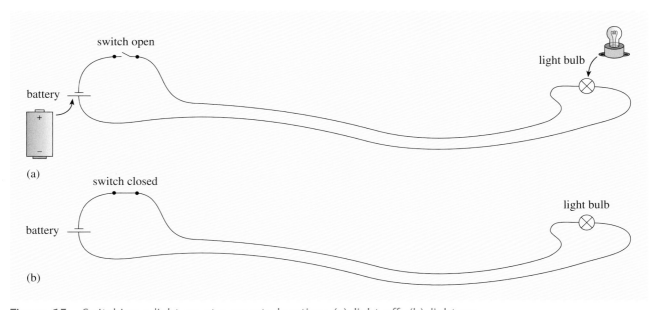

Figure 15   Switching a light on at a remote location: (a) light off; (b) light on

When you switch a light on, the light appears to come on immediately. There does not appear to be any delay between operating the switch and the effect at the light (although, depending on the type of light there might be a delay before it comes on fully – this is especially noticeable with fluorescent light tubes). In reality there is a delay – it is just very short indeed.

To get a better insight into what is happening, imagine measuring the voltage between the wires. This can be done with something called a **voltmeter** (Figure 16). A voltmeter has two wires and a display. When you touch the ends of the wires to the terminals of a power source like a battery, the display on the meter tells you what the voltage is between the terminals.

voltmeter

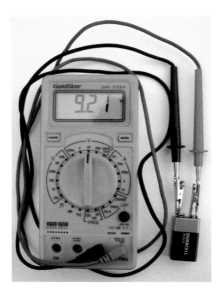

Figure 16 A voltmeter

Imagine using the voltmeter to measure the voltage between the two wires at some point between the switch and the light, as in Figure 17. When the switch is open (off) the reading on the meter will be zero. When the switch is closed (on), the reading will (ideally) be equal to the voltage of the battery – which I shall assume is 1.2 volts. Now imagine having the voltmeter touching the wires while the switch is changed from open to closed. In this case you will see the voltage change from 0 to 1.2 V.

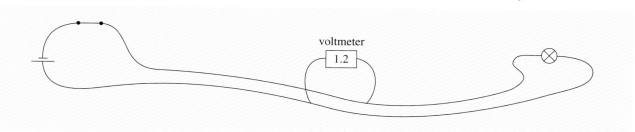

Figure 17 Measuring the voltage across a pair of wires

Now, if the voltmeter is touching the wires right next to the switch, you would see the voltage rise from 0 to 1.2 V at the same instant as the switch is closed. If, on the other hand, the voltmeter is touching the wires further away from the switch there will be a delay between the switch closing and the voltage rising. We can display this by plotting graphs as shown in Figure 18.

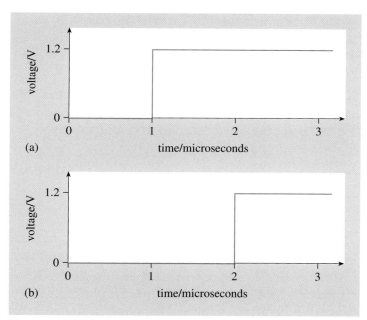

Figure 18 The voltage across wires when a switch is closed: (a) voltage across the wires as measured at the switch; (b) voltage across the wires as measured 200 m away from the switch

These graphs show how the reading on the voltmeter changes with time. Along the horizontal axis from left to right corresponds to time passing, and up the vertical axis corresponds to increasing voltage, as measured by the voltmeter. The time axis is labelled in units of microseconds, where one microsecond is one-millionth of a second. Notice also that the time axis is relative to some time origin which is labelled 0. The actual time corresponding to 0 as shown on the axis might have been, say, Thursday 20 May 2004, 2.17 pm and 35.031233

By convention, the axis that goes across the page is the 'horizontal' axis, and the axis that goes up and down the page is the 'vertical' axis. Sometimes they are called the x and y axes, for horizontal and vertical respectively.

seconds, but labelling the axis with that level of detail would be confusing and irrelevant.

Figure 18(a) shows what the voltmeter would do when connected to the wires next to the switch, while Figure 18(b) shows what it would do when connected to the wires 200 m along towards the light bulb. The switch was closed at time 1, on this scale, so the voltage measured next to the switch rises at time 1.

There is a delay before the voltage rises at the voltmeter when it is 200 m along the wire.

Activity 28 (exploratory)

How much of a delay?

Comment

The voltage rises when the time is equal to 2 microseconds. The switch was closed at a time equal to 1 microsecond, so there is a one-microsecond delay between the switch being closed and the voltage changing 200 m along the wire.

We can think of the change in voltage moving along the wires. This idea of the change in voltage moving along the wire becomes clear if we think about turning the light on and then off again afterwards. This is illustrated in Figure 19.

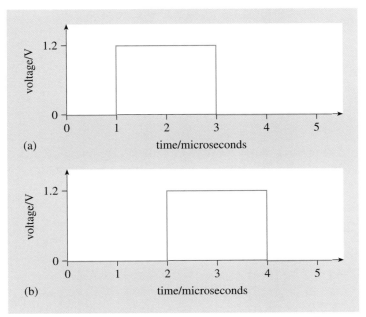

Figure 19 A voltage pulse travelling along a pair of wires: (a) voltage across the wires as measured at the switch; (b) voltage across the wires as measured 200 m away from the switch

Here, the switch is closed at time 1 microsecond and opened again at time 3 microseconds. We now have a *voltage pulse*. Looking at the voltage across the wires 200 m from the switch, both the rise and fall in voltage happen 1 microsecond later, and the voltage pulse has taken 1 microsecond to travel the 200 m along the wires.

Activity 29 (exploratory)

How fast is the pulse travelling, measured in metres per second?

Comment

The pulse travels 200 metres in 1 microsecond. 1 microsecond is one-millionth of a second, so in 1 second it would travel 200×1 million metres = 200 million metres or 2×10^8 metres. The speed is therefore 2×10^8 m/s.

This is two-thirds of the speed of light, which is typical of the speed that electric signals travel along wires.

Activity 30 (self-assessment)

Assuming that the pulse continues to travel at the same speed, draw a graph of voltage against time for measurements taken 600 metres from the switch.

Comment

The answer is at the end of this part.

Figures 18 and 19 (and my answer to Activity 30) are simplifications because they have not shown attenuation or distortion. Figure 20 shows the sort of effects that attenuation and distortion might have on a pulse.

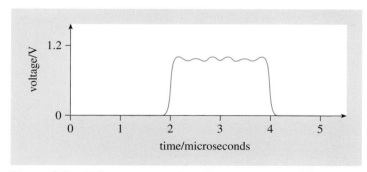

Figure 20 Voltage across the wires as measured 200 m away from the switch, showing the effects of attenuation and distortion

I now say 'look at the voltage' rather than 'the value on the voltmeter'. I only introduced the idea of the (idealised) voltmeter to set up the concept of the voltage having a value at some place on the wires.

Attenuation reduces the height of the pulse, so that it does not reach 1.2 volts any more. Some of the voltage has been 'lost' as it travels the 200 metres because some energy from the electricity is absorbed by (very slightly) heating the wires and some energy is radiated into the air as the wires act as a (very inefficient) aerial.

Distortion alters the pulse, rounding the corners and generally changing the shape. Qualitatively, the smoothing of the corners is because the wires do not allow the voltage to change instantaneously – there is a sort of electrical drag as the pulse travels along the wires. More random distortion effects are caused by what is referred to as **noise**. By analogy with the common meaning of noise as unwanted, meaningless sounds, noise in the context of electrical signals is the unavoidable effect where signals develop unwanted, meaningless distortions.

noise

Attenuation and distortion become worse as the pulse travels further. Amplifiers can be used to compensate for attenuation, but that still leaves distortion, which ultimately limits how far signals can be transmitted along a wire – or indeed any transmission medium. With digital signals, however, **regenerators** can be used instead of (or as well as) amplifiers to overcome both attenuation and distortion.

regenerator

The concept of regeneration is that when a pulse has become badly attenuated or distorted, it can be regenerated to produce a new, perfect pulse for onward transmission. This is illustrated in Figure 21. Note that to simplify the diagram I have drawn a single line to represent a pair of wires. The pulses drawn next to the line represent pulses across the pair of wires at that location.

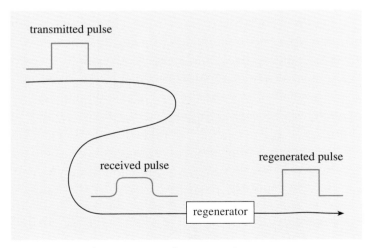

Figure 21   The concept of regeneration

You do not need to know how regeneration is done in detail; you just need to understand that it is possible. The reason it is possible is that with digital signals there is a restricted range of possibilities of what the signal could be. For example, with a binary signal, 1s and 0s might be

transmitted on wire by using, say, 5 V to represent a 1 and 0 V to represent a 0. The regenerator 'knows' that the only signal it is expecting is something which started out either as a pulse of 5 V or as 0 V. The regenerator decides which of the two possibilities is most likely, and produces a new 5 V pulse or 0 V accordingly. Although there are practical complications, in principle this decision can be very simple. An electrical circuit compares the received voltage with a threshold value (say 2.5 V) and if the received voltage is greater than the threshold the output is a new 5 V pulse, otherwise the output is 0 V.

Ideally, regeneration can be repeated indefinitely allowing transmission over unlimited distances (Figure 22).

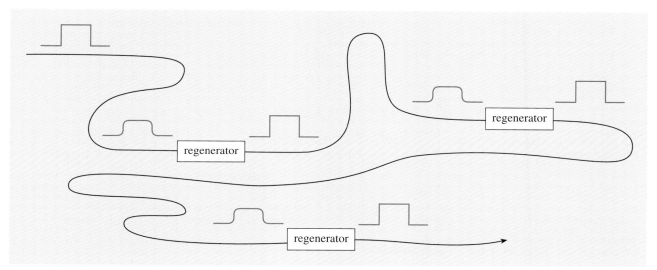

Figure 22 Successive regeneration for long-distance transmission

The boxes labelled 'regenerator' in Figure 22 are electronic circuits, but interestingly the very first 'regenerators' were human beings! Early electric telegraph systems operated by the opening and closing of a switch at the transmitter having the effect of a pen putting marks on a piece of paper at the receiver. These were digital systems, with 'marks' and 'spaces' on the paper performing a similar role to 0s and 1s in modern digital systems. In telegraph relay stations, telegraph operators (people) would look at the marks and spaces on an incoming telegraph line and duplicate them on an outgoing telegraph to send the message on the next leg of its journey.

5.2   Other transmission media

Wires are still used to carry electrical signals over short distances. At the time of writing, for example, most connections between telephones in private houses and the local telephone exchange still use wires. The telephone networks within office buildings are mostly connected with

wires, and so are many computer networks (local area networks, LANs) within single buildings. However, all longer-distance communication, between towns, cities or countries, uses either optical fibre or microwave systems. Increasingly, even shorter distances use either optical fibres or wireless links of one sort or another.

Many of the concepts described in the previous section for signal transmission on electrical wires also apply to wireless systems (such as microwave) or optical fibres. Pulses are still attenuated and distorted, for example. It is worth, however, briefly looking at some of the characteristics particular to these other transmission media.

Microwave

You saw the importance of microwave transmission for newsgathering in the Higgins extract. The term 'microwave' identifies a particular range of frequencies used for radio communications. The range of frequencies that are referred to as 'microwave' is not exactly defined (or, rather, slightly different ranges are used in different contexts), but roughly speaking it is from about 200 MHz to 50 GHz.

It is possible to transmit digital signals over microwave by using pulses of microwave power to represent 1s, and the absence of microwave power to represent 0s. This type of transmission is known as on-off keying. In practice this is not generally the best way to use microwave for transmission, and more sophisticated ways of putting the data on the radio signal (different **modulation schemes**) are normally used.

Regeneration is used in microwave transmission systems, but surprisingly long distances are possible without regeneration. In satellite communications the satellite performs regeneration (as well as some other functions), but that still means that the signal has to travel the distance from the ground to the satellite in one go (and the same distance back). For geostationary satellites this is 36 000 km each way.

Even more remarkable is the microwave transmission that was used to send data back from the Cassini–Huygens space exploration mission to Saturn and its moon, Titan, in 2004/05. The distance between the Earth and Saturn was at that time 1 517 000 000 km! The reduction in the signal strength over that distance is very great, so the power of the signal received back on the Earth is small. In practice this means that the data rate (bandwidth) is small, because there is a trade-off between signal power and data rate. For high data rates higher power is needed. If the power is low, only low data rates are possible. (It is the same if you are having difficulty hearing someone speaking, when you might ask them to speak more slowly.)

Optical fibre

In all developed countries, long-distance communication links (which used to be called 'trunks', by analogy to 'trunk road') nearly always use

Remember that MHz stands for megahertz, which is 1 000 000 Hz (10^6 Hz) and GHz is gigahertz, which is 1 000 000 000 Hz (10^9 Hz).

modulation scheme

optical fibre. It is only where the terrain makes it difficult to lay a cable (such as in mountains or, sometimes, between islands) or when a new link is needed quickly and there isn't time to lay a cable that microwave links are used instead.

An optical fibre is a strand of glass or plastic, not much thicker than a human hair, which guides light from one end to the other (Figure 23). The guidance comes about because of an effect known as total internal reflection. This means that light shone in one end of the fibre doesn't come out from the sides of the fibre even if the fibre is bent around corners. The light just travels inside the fibre until it comes to the far end. Because the fibre is so thin it is flexible and, from the outside of a cable with protective plastic coverings, looks and feels much the same as an electrical wire. Signals are conveyed by changing the 'brightness' of the light injected into the fibre and measuring it at the far end. Bits are sent by 'on-off keying': 1s are represented by light on and 0s by light off.

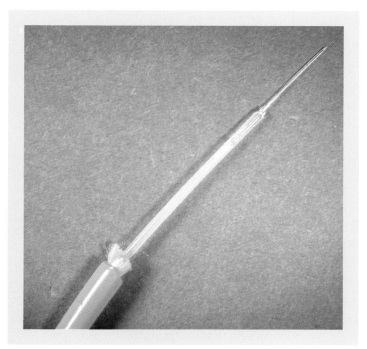

Figure 23 Optical fibre of the type used for communications. The bare glass fibre is vulnerable to scratches and will break if bent too tightly, so the cable shown has several layers of protective coverings, shown here stripped off layer by layer.

The attraction of optical fibre is that it can be used for very high data rates over long distances. It is this combination – high data rates and long distances – that distiguishes it from wires.

When electrical signals are transmitted over wires the attenuation increases with increasing data rate, so the higher the data rate, the greater the attenuation and therefore the shorter the distance that can

be used. So, for example, although signals at 1 gigabit/s can be carried around on wires inside a computer, it is difficult to transmit electrical signals even a few metres at data rates that high. With optical fibre the attenuation is not dependent on the data rate, and the attenuation is anyway very low, so that signals at tens or even hundreds of gigabit/s can be sent for tens of kilometres with the right sort of fibre.

There are other factors to consider, including, as mentioned above, that higher data rates require higher power (which is the case whatever the medium used to carry the signal). Nevertheless, even though optical fibre is generally more expensive to use than wires, optical fibre is the transmission medium to use for high data rates over long distances.

Activity 31 (exploratory)

When optical fibre was first developed as a communications medium, it was initially used only for long-distance transmission between cities. More recently it has been used for shorter distances, including many new local area networks (LANs) within office buildings. There is also a debate about how and when it should be used in the links between private homes and the local telephone exchange. From the discussion above, can you suggest why it is now finding applications for shorter distances, where metallic wires were previously used?

Comment

In recent years the data rates required of many communication links have been increasing. Since the attenuation of wires increases with increasing data rates, many links which previously could use wires cannot do so any more, because the data rates are too high. Where data rates have got too high to use wires, optical fibre is often used instead.

Also, although this was not discussed in the text, the equipment needed for optical fibre transmission has been getting cheaper, making its use more economical in a variety of applications.

5.3   Signal speeds, propagation times and distance: the formula triangle

When signals travel along a wire or optical fibre, or through space, the relationship between the speed, propagation time and distance can be written in three ways, depending upon which one you want to calculate.

If you know the speed and the propagation time and want to know how far the signal will travel, you use:

distance = propagation time × speed

You should recall that this is the calculation I used for the active autofocusing in Section 4.1.

I shall use d for the distance and t for the time, as I did earlier. For speed I shall follow the common convention of using v, which comes from 'velocity' – but you have to be careful not to get confused with v for voltage, as used in Section 4.3.

So, we have:

$$d = t\,v$$

If you know the distance travelled and speed but want to calculate the propagation time you use:

$$\text{propagation time} = \frac{\text{distance}}{\text{speed}}$$

Technically the value for the velocity of something includes both its speed and the direction it is moving in. For our purposes there is no need to distinguish between speed and velocity. I shall just use the word speed and the symbol v.

which can be written:

$$t = \frac{d}{v}$$

Finally, if you know the distance travelled and the propagation time, and want to calculate the speed, you use:

$$\text{speed} = \frac{\text{distance}}{\text{propagation time}}$$

or

$$v = \frac{d}{t}$$

These are of course quite general relationships between distance travelled, time taken and speed. We used the same relationship when doing the calculations for autofocusing in a camcorder, and it applies equally for the journey time driving along a motorway or cycling to work, assuming constant speed (or using average speed in the calculation). The relationship between these three terms is displayed on a formula triangle as shown in Figure 24. You can swap the 'time' (t) and 'speed' (v) in the lower corners – it doesn't matter which way round these are.

Earlier I explained how you draw the formula triangle given one of the equations, but what is useful about the triangle is that you can get back to any of the equations from the triangle.

You do this by covering the quantity you want to calculate, and looking at the position of the other two (Figure 25). So if you want to calculate the time, you cover 'time' and observe that distance appears above

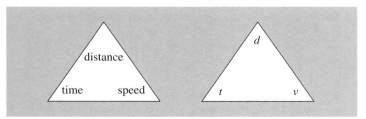

Figure 24   The formula triangle

speed, so you calculate time from distance divided by speed. Similarly, to calculate speed, you cover 'speed' and observe that distance appears above time so you divide distance by time. For calculating distance, you cover 'distance' and note that time is alongside speed, so you multiply the two together.

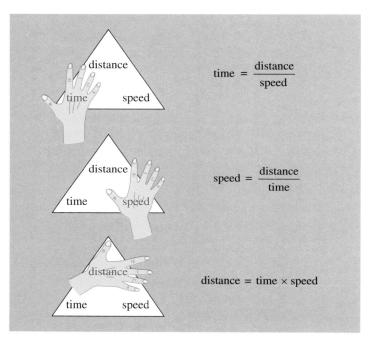

Figure 25   Using the formula triangle

Activity 32 (self-assessment)

In Activity 23 you drew a formula triangle for the relationship between battery capacity, current (i) and the length of time a battery can be used (t).

(a) Suppose you know the battery capacity and the time you want to use the battery for. Write down the formula which will allow you to calculate the current. Use the formula triangle to help you.

(b) Suppose a battery has a capacity of 1.8 Ah and is to be used for 20 hours. What is the maximum current that can be drawn from it?

Comment

The answer is at the end of this part.

It is important when doing the calculations that you use consistent units. You could use the standard units known as SI units (see box), but you don't have to, so long as the units are consistent. For example, if you have speed in kilometres per hour and time in hours, then distance will be in kilometres.

SI units

One way of ensuring that you are working with consistent units is to use the international standard units known as 'SI' units, where SI stands for the French words Système International. The SI unit for length is the metre and for time is the second. In SI units, therefore, speed is expressed as metres per second. There is more about SI units in *The Sciences Good Study Guide* (Northedge et al., 1997).

Activity 33 (exploratory)

For a communications satellite to be in a geostationary orbit it has to be about 36 000 km above the Earth. How much delay will be introduced to a radio signal by having to go up to and back down from the satellite? Radio signals travel at the speed of light (3×10^8 m/s), and you should assume that the signals go straight up and straight down. Note that this assumption – straight up and straight down – simplifies the calculation, and means that you get a value that would be an underestimate to the delay, for all cases except where the communication really is straight up and down (see Figure 26). In practice, communication via the satellite will often use an angled path and therefore have a larger delay.

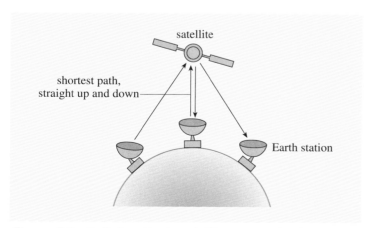

Figure 26   Path lengths in satellite communications

Comment

We need the time, so we use:

$$\text{Propagation time} = \frac{\text{distance}}{\text{speed}}$$

We first write the distance and speed in consistent units. The speed is in units of metres per second (3×10^8 m/s) but the distance is in kilometres (36 000 km). The multiplier 'kilo' is $\times 1000$, so in metres the distance is $36\,000 \times 1000$ m $= 36\,000\,000$ m $= 3.6 \times 10^7$ m. This is the distance to or from the satellite. One 'hop' – up and down – is twice this distance, 7.2×10^7 m.

So we have:

$$\text{Propagation time (delay)} = \frac{7.2 \times 10^7}{3 \times 10^8}\,\text{s} = \frac{72\,000\,000}{300\,000\,000} = 0.24\,\text{s}$$

You might think that 0.24 seconds (about a quarter of a second) is not very long, but in fact if you were having a conversation with someone and there was a delay this long, it would be quite noticeable – and something of a nuisance. When you say something then stop to wait for a reply, it takes a quarter of a second for what you say to reach the other person, then there is another quarter of a second delay before the reply reaches you. So, in total, there is half a second delay (in addition to the recipient deciding what to say) between you finishing what you say and hearing the reply.

Activity 34 (self-assessment)

Satellites are frequently used for transatlantic communication, but the alternative is to use undersea cables. These days undersea cables would invariably use optical fibre. Light in fibre travels at about 2/3 of the speed of light in the air (light travels more slowly in glass than in the air) and therefore the signal speed is about 2×10^8 m/s. The distance across the Atlantic (depending upon where you start and finish) is about 4000 km. How long does it take for a signal to cross the Atlantic travelling through optical fibre?

Comment

The answer is at the end of this part.

You will have seen from the last activity that the delay when using optical fibre is very much less than when using a geostationary satellite. This is not the whole story, because there may be further delays when signals are manipulated (which can happen both with satellites and optical fibre links), but nevertheless it remains true that in speech telephony there is a noticeable delay when the communication uses a

geostationary satellite, but not, usually, when it uses a fibre link. Delays used to be commonly encountered when you telephoned the USA from the UK, but that is rare these days because most transatlantic calls are via optical fibre links. It is important to appreciate that the large delay when using geostationary satellites comes about because geostationary satellites are so far from the Earth. Other satellites are also used whose orbits are much closer to the Earth. Communication via these non-geostationary satellites can have a smaller delay, but there are other complications because the satellite is moving relative to the Earth's surface.

As you saw in the Taylor extract in Section 2, news broadcasts often use geostationary satellites and therefore suffer from the larger delay. The processing (manipulation) used in MPEG encoding, especially motion compensation, adds yet more delay. The combined delays of transmission and processing can cause problems for live news broadcasts, as Higgins discusses later in his book:

MPEG coding was discussed in Part 1 of this block.

> The interaction in a 'live' two-way interview requires that both the questions and answers are delivered as smoothly as possible, but the delay of the compression process which is then added to the fixed satellite delay means that these interviews often have an awkward hesitancy about them.
>
> This can be masked to a degree by imaginative techniques used both in the studio and out in the field, but there is always the evident hesitation between interviewer and interviewee. These compression delays ('latency') have reduced as the computational advances in processing speed have increased.
>
> The viewer is also growing more tolerant of these delays to the point where they are hardly noticed, and so the problems are diminishing as time passes.
>
> Some coders also offer a facility to improve the latency at the expense of movement compensation [motion compensation] – the so-called interview or low-delay mode. This is selected via the front panel menu of the MPEG-2 coder, reducing the overall processing time of the signal.
>
> Changing production techniques is by far the best way to try to overcome these awkward pauses. It is common for the studio to cue the reporter a fraction of a second earlier than normal, so that by the time they respond, the delay has passed unnoticed.
>
> Often you will see reporters in the field looking thoughtful or slowly nodding after they have replied to a question, so that it makes their eventual answer to the next question look as if it is a very carefully considered reply! Like many other things in TV, much can be achieved by using 'smoke and mirrors'!

These techniques of course do not work if it is a straight 'down the line' interview with a member of the public, who naturally is unaware of these tricks of the trade.

However, you can often see this all going horribly wrong even with a seasoned reporter if there is a studio presenter asking questions who does not appreciate the subtle techniques required to cope with satellite and compression delay.

Classically this happens when part way through the answer from a reporter in the field, the presenter interjects with a supplementary question or comment. The field reporter carries on for a second or so, then halts in their tracks, meanwhile the studio presenter realises their mistake and urges the reporter in the field to continue – and you get a cycle of each end saying 'Sorry, please go on'.

This was a lesson that had to be learnt in the early days of satellite broadcasting which became more acute when digital processing and encoding was introduced – yet you still see these problems occurring today.

Higgins (2004)

6 Trust

Information is worthless if you have no trust in it. This has always been the case, but there are issues of trust that arise specifically in the context of modern information and communication technologies. Think about the following:

- You do a search on the Web and get results from several different sites. Do you trust the information in them all? How do you decide which are the most trustworthy?

- You get an email, a letter or a phone call purporting to come from your bank, recommending a change to your account. Do you follow the advice that you are given?

- You read a story in a newspaper, hear it on the radio or see it on TV. Do you believe it? Does it make any difference if it is accompanied by a photograph?

- In each of these cases there are two elements to your trust:

    1   The authority of the information source. Do you trust the BBC, ITN or someone you've never met writing a weblog? The *Guardian* or the *Daily Mail*? Your bank?

    2   Authentication of the message – does it really come from whom you think it does? Is it really the BBC's website you are looking at? Does this person writing a weblog really live in Iraq? Is the email, phone call or letter really from your bank?

Authority of OU teaching material

It may be dangerous to raise this question ... but do you trust what you read in OU courses? What grounds are there for trusting us?

I hope that you do trust the OU – but not unquestioningly, because we do get things wrong sometimes. The Open University 'brand' comes with some authority, and there are mechanisms within the University procedures to ensure the quality of OU material. These procedures include:

- Team working. This block, for example, has emerged from course team discussions, and drafts which have been read and criticised by the whole course team.

- External consultants. Experts from outside the University are asked for advice and contribute in various ways.

- External assessors and examiners. OU regulations require that senior academics from other universities approve courses both during the production phase and annually during the course's presentation.

Further procedures operate at higher levels within the OU structure and formally the quality of all university education in the UK is monitored by the QAA: Quality Assurance Authority for Higher Education (see http://www.qaa.ac.uk/).

It must also not be forgotten that when the course is in presentation large numbers of Associate Lecturers and students read the material and provide feedback if they identify problems.

6.1   Authority and the variety of information sources

Technology has massively increased the number and variety of news sources that we have access to. We still have printed books, magazines and newspapers, while digital techniques have increased the number of broadcast radio and TV channels that we can get. On the Web we have access to online versions of many of these – see the online material associated with this block for links to online newspapers and radio, for example. This allows us access to media that previously would have been inaccessible.

With traditional news sources such as these, we have some understanding of the authority that they bring with them. Newspapers, for example, rely to some extent on their reputation. This may be damaged – they might lose readers – if their stories are found to be wrong or misleading, so it is in their own interests to maintain standards. Also, in the UK, newspapers and magazines are regulated by the Press Complaints Commission, the PCC. There are similar considerations that apply to radio and TV to maintain standards. In all these cases there will be some degree of editorial control over the content, and one of the responsibilities of the editors is to maintain standards of honesty appropriate to their publication or channel.

On the internet, however, there are sources of news and information that are completely unregulated. The technology is such that with a minimum of knowledge and little expense, virtually anyone (in the developed world anyway) can say almost anything they like on a personal web page or a weblog, and, in principle at least, their words are instantly available to millions of people all over the world. The absence of any regulation or external editorial control might be thought to devalue personal web pages or weblogs as sources of news, but there are other considerations. To what extent do websites gain authority by the number of other sites that link to them, and by who links to them? Can personal recommendations replace recognised authorisation? And anyway, perhaps regulation sometimes becomes censorship, and who has the right to determine the editorial 'line'?

The PCC is a form of self-regulation rather than statutory regulation (regulation by law), and some people argue that this is inadequate.

I raise these questions because they highlight issues that arise from the development of the Web, but there are no simple answers. We can gain some insight into the issues involved, however, by looking at one particular example where a weblog was able to provide news that was simply not available through any other source.

The example that I shall use is that of the 'Baghdad Blogger', Salam Pax, who was posting reports from Baghdad in the run-up to, and all through, the 2003 war in Iraq. As the US and British troops advanced on Iraq, news was coming from several sources, most of which might be suspected to be censored in some way. Salam was a resident of Baghdad who did not set out to be a reporter, but whose interest in the Web led him to create a weblog that became seen by many as providing a valuable insight into life in Baghdad at this time.

In the article below (itself taken from one of the traditional news sources: the *Guardian* newspaper), Salam Pax (2003) writes about his experiences. As you read it, think about some of the questions that I asked earlier, but also notice the role of the technology.

Higgins, in his book that we quoted from earlier (*Introduction to SNG and ENG Microwave*), writes some fascinating descriptions of journalists setting up microwave links to report from the Iraq war zone. We do not have space to reproduce them here, but if you are interested you could buy or borrow the book from a library yourself.

'I Became The Profane Pervert Arab Blogger'

S. Pax

9 September, 2003

The Guardian

My name is Salam Pax and I am addicted to blogs. Some people watch daytime soaps, I follow blogs. I follow the hyperlinks on the blogs I read. I travel through the web guided by bloggers. I get wrapped up in the plots narrated by them. [...]

We [the Iraqi people] had no access to satellite TV, and magazines had to be smuggled into the country. Through blogs I could take a peek at a different world. Satellite TV and the web were on Saddam's list of things that will corrupt you. Having a satellite dish was punishable with jail and a hefty fine [...]

While the world was moving on to high-speed internet, we were being told it was overrated. So when in 2000 the first state-operated internet centre was opened, everybody was a bit suspicious, no one knew if browsing news sites would get you in trouble. When, another year later, you were able to get access from home, life changed. We had internet and we were able to browse without the minders at the internet centres watching over our shoulder, asking you what that site you are browsing is.

Of course things were not that easy, there was a firewall. A black page with big orange letters: access denied. They made you sign a paper which said you would not try to get to sites which were of an 'unfriendly' nature and that you would report these sites to the administrator. They blocked certain search terms and they did actually have a bunch of people looking at URL requests going through their servers. It sounds absurd but believe me, they did that. I had a friend who worked at the ISP and he would tell me about the latest trouble in the Mukhabarat [secret police] room.

[...] With blogs the web started talking to me in a much more personal way. Bits of news started having texture and most amazingly, these blogs talked with each other. That hyperlink to the next blog – I just couldn't stop clicking. [...]

To tell you the truth, sharing with the world wasn't really that high on my top five reasons to start a blog. It was more about sharing with Raed, my Jordanian friend who went to Amman after we finished architecture school in Baghdad. He is a lousy email writer; you just don't expect any answers from him. [...]. So instead of writing emails and then having to dig them up later it would all be there on the blog. So Where is Raed? started. [...]

The first reckless thing I did was to put the blog address in a blog indexing site under Iraq. I did this after I spent a couple of days searching for Arabs

blogging and finding mostly religious blogs. I thought the Arab world deserved a fair representation in the blogsphere, and decided that I would be the profane pervert Arab blogger just in case someone was looking.

Putting my site at that portal (eatonweb) was the beginning of the changing of my blog's nature. I got linked by the Legendary Monkey and then Instapundit – a blog that can drive a stampede of traffic to your site. I saw my site counter jump from the usual 20 hits a day to 3,000, all coming from Instapundit – we call it experiencing an Insta-lanche (from avalanche) [...]

What really worried me was the people writing those emails were doing so as if I was a spokesman for the Iraqi people. There are 25 million Iraqis and I am just one. With the attention came the fear that someone in Iraq might actually read the blog, since by now it had entered warblog territory. But Mr Site Killer still didn't block it. I preferred to believe they were not watching. They were never patient. If they knew about it I would already have been hanging from a ceiling being asked about anti-governmental activities. Real trouble comes when big media takes notice and this happened when there was a mention of the blog and its URL in a Reuters piece [...]

By the end of January war felt very close and the blog was being read by a huge number of people. There were big doubts that I was writing from Baghdad, the main argument being there was no way such a thing could stay under the radar for so long in a police state. I really have no idea how that happened. I have no idea whether they knew about it or not. I just felt that it was important that among all the weblogs about Iraq and the war there should be at least one Iraqi blog, one single voice: no matter how you view my politics, there was at least someone talking.

I was sometimes really angry at the various articles in the press telling the world about how Iraqis feel and what they were doing when they were living in an isolated world. The journalists could not talk to people in the street without a Mukhabarat man standing beside them. As the war came closer, my blog started getting mentioned more and more. There were people quoting it even after I told them not to, because I feared it would attract too much attention. I talked to as few people as possible and did not answer any interview requests, but my blog was popping up in all sorts of publications. The questions people were asking me became more difficult and the amount of angry mail I was getting became unbelievable. Raed thought I should start panicking. People wanted coherence and a clear stand for or against war. All I had was doubt and uncertainty.

[...]

Activity 35 (exploratory)

. . . .

(a) One issue with weblogs as a source of news is that they present just one individual's perception of events, arguably with no more authority to speak than anyone else. Salam makes two apparently contradictory statements about this issue in the article. Pick out these two statements.

(b) What was it that led to a sudden increase in the number of people looking at Salam's website?

(c) What might lead you to trust the content of Salam Pax's blog?

Comment

(a) The two statements that I picked out are:

'What really worried me was the people writing those emails were doing so as if I was a spokesman for the Iraqi people. There are 25 million Iraqis and I am just one.'

and

'I just felt that it was important that among all the weblogs about Iraq and the war there should be at least one Iraqi blog, one single voice: no matter how you view my politics, there was at least someone talking.'

These seem to be contradictory, but maybe there just isn't a simple answer.

(b) Salam says that the number of 'hits' on his blog – the number of times someone looked at his site – rose from 20 per day to 3000 following his site being linked by 'Legendary Monkey and then Instapundit'. Specifically, he says that the 3000 were all coming from Instapundit.

(c) The fact that other people and organisations, whom you already trust, are implicitly or explicitly endorsing Salam Pax's blog might give you confidence in it. It seems that 'Instapundit' already had the confidence of many people when it provided a link to 'Where is Raed?', and its being mentioned by Reuters would have given it some authority. Personally, it was when it appeared in the *Guardian* that I first came across it, and I assumed that the *Guardian* would have made some checks on its authenticity.

6.2   Authentication of information

When I watch TV news, listen to the radio or buy a newspaper I never think to question whether I really am watching ITV, listening to Radio Five-Live or getting the *Guardian*. In each of these cases it is theoretically possible that they are not who they say they are, but the practicalities of performing the masquerade are so complicated that the possibility can be discarded.

With emails and websites it is a very different matter. Indeed, in recent months I have received several emails apparently coming from organisations, such as Microsoft and NatWest bank, which I know were fake. They looked entirely authentic, with the correct graphics, and the first time I received one of these – apparently from Microsoft – at first sight I was taken in. However, from other sources of information I learned that 'scams' such as these were in circulation and Microsoft and the major banks have said that they will never use emails to ask for personal information.

The authentic appearance of the emails was meaningless, since it is almost trivially easy to copy images from websites and paste them elsewhere, such as into emails. Incoming telephone calls are equally suspect, and again there have been cases of scams whereby a caller claims to be from somewhere they are not.

Letters with official documents have in the past been more reliable, since it was difficult to reproduce headed notepaper accurately. It is still possible to generate official documents that are hard to imitate (through the use of watermarks or embossing, for example) but the availability of high-quality colour printers has made it easier to produce official-looking documents.

Activity 36 (exploratory)

Suppose you are contacted by email, telephone or letter and you want to check whether the communication is authentic. What could you do?

Comment

If you already have a contact number for the organisation that has contacted you, you could call them and ask about it. This only works, of course, if you already have the number which you know is correct. Email scams often contain a phone number, but that number is, of course, bogus.

A personal signature on a letter changes the situation, provided you know the signature, can recognise it and it isn't a photocopy. The signature is the **authentication** of the letter. Similarly, recognising the voice of someone on the telephone authenticates the call. Authentication of emails is also possible by the use of **digital signatures**. A digital signature is a special piece of data which is added to a message. Software on the recipient's computer can analyse the message and the signature and determine whether the message is authentic. Digital signatures only work if your computer already 'knows' about the sender.

authentication

digital signature

The technology of digital signatures can be used to authenticate websites as well as emails. In this case, your web browser checks the **certificate** of the site. This is usually done automatically, with your browser reporting to you if there is a problem.

certificate

6.3 Pictures

It used to be thought that a photograph could provide proof of an event – someone could be caught red-handed by a photograph, as proof of their guilt. 'The camera never lies', it was said. If you have a digital camera and have been 'touching up' photographs on your home computer you will know that this is far from true now. It is easy to lie with a digital photograph.

The idea that the camera never lies has always been a myth, however. As far back as 1917 the photographs of the Cottingley fairies 'proved' the existence of fairies. Two girls, Elsie Wright (age 16) and Frances Griffiths (age 9), took photographs of themselves apparently in the company of fairies (Figure 27). Eventually, in 1981, the girls admitted that they had faked most of the pictures – although they always maintained that one of them was genuine.

Figure 27 The Cottingley Fairies

The difference today is the ease with which digital photographs can be manipulated. It is argued that because of this, digital photography is qualitatively different from analogue photography.

One of the benefits that Taylor claimed for digital techniques is the improved options for editing, and he contrasted digital techniques with analogue techniques where 'stories cannot easily be altered'. The counterpoint to this is that digital stories *can* be easily altered – which makes them all the more unreliable.

This has sparked a debate about the changing nature of photography. The artist David Hockney, who has used photography in his work, has

argued that the ease of editing digital images has made photography a dying art. Hockney's views were discussed in a newspaper article in 2004.

> Hockney says he believes modern photography is now so extensively and easily altered that it can no longer be seen to be true or factual. He also describes art photography as 'dull'.
>
> Even war photography, once seen as objectively 'true', has now been cast in doubt by the ubiquitous use of digital cameras which produce images that can be easily enhanced or twisted.
>
> Hockney points to the case during the Iraq war when the *Los Angeles Times* sacked a photographer for having superimposed two images to make them more powerful.
>
> Jones and Seenan (2004)

Not everyone entirely agrees.

> Russell Roberts, head of photography at the National Museum of Photography, Film and Television, said Hockney's argument was 'simplistic'.
>
> Mr Roberts said manipulation of images was as old as photography. He could cite numerous examples from the 1840s, the first decade of photography, of images which claimed to be accurate depictions of events but were in fact highly stage managed.
>
> [...]
>
> Eamonn McCabe, a former picture editor of the *Guardian*, said it had become increasingly difficult for picture editors to tell whether a picture had been manipulated and a growing number of digitally manipulated pictures were being published.
>
> 'I think there was perhaps a point where there was a general perception that photography was truth, but we have lost that,' he said.
>
> But McCabe said this did not detract from the value of good photography. 'To say that photography is dead is faintly ludicrous. It would be better to say that you should be wary of everything.'
>
> Jones and Seenan (2004)

McCabe's measured response to the consequences of digital photography, in contrast to Hockney's more sensational reaction, echos the discussion earlier in this block (Section 1 of Part 1) when you were asked to compare recent claims made about ICTs with past claims made about telegraph, films and electricity. It was suggested that you should

be wary of exaggerated, utopian claims about the power of technologies. Likewise you should watch out for exaggeration in claims of the negative consequences of technology. Certainly ICTs have made significant changes in many areas of our lives: that is what T175 is all about. I hope, however, that your study of T175 puts you in a more powerful position to think critically about ICTs, and make informed judgements on the consequences of new information and communication technologies.

7 Summary of Block 3 Part 2

The theme of this part of Block 3 has been the impact that information and communication technologies have had on the news industry. I introduced this theme with a short historical overview of technology in the news industry followed by a look at how technology is used for newsgathering.

We have been looking in some detail at aspects of the underlying technologies used in newsgathering, including the basic components of digital camcorders and the methods of signal transmission over wires. We have used some mathematical methods, with a particular emphasis on equations that can be represented with a formula triangle. We have also explored some basic ideas about electricity in the context of the batteries that are needed to supply the power for portable ICT equipment.

Finally we have considered the issue of trust in information, and the way in which recent ICTs have required us to think again about what enables us to trust information.

ANSWERS TO SELF-ASSESSMENT ACTIVITIES

Activity 2

(a) Digital compression reduces the number of bits needed to store or transmit digitally encoded data. This means, for example, that a video server of a given size will be able to store more video (more and/or longer video sequences) if it is compressed than if it is uncompressed.

(b) The MPEG standards are commonly used for compressing digital video signals.

Activity 3

Runlength coding compresses binary data by replacing long runs of bits that are all the same (long runs of 1s or long runs of 0s) by codes that state how long the runs are. Since it takes fewer bits to transmit a message saying that, for example, there is a run of 200 bits all having the value one than to transmit 200 ones, runlength coding can reduce the amount of data needed to transmit a file which contains runs like this.

Activity 5

From what Taylor says, it seems that the equipment needed for the 16 mm film was cheaper, lighter and more manageable than that needed for the 35 mm. Using 16 mm film therefore allowed ITN to have moving pictures with more of their stories.

Activity 6

Taylor says of the development of the Hawkeye camcorder:

> This development sparked the imagination of news broadcasters who quickly recognised the benefits of getting away from film with all its processing delays and bulky, expensive telecine equipment and of course its inability to provide live coverage.
>
> Taylor (1995)

In other words, the disadvantages of film were that:

- there were processing delays
- the equipment needed to convert from film to electronic video for broadcasting (the telecine equipment) was expensive and bulky
- it could not be used for live coverage.

Activity 7

My answer is shown in Figure 28.

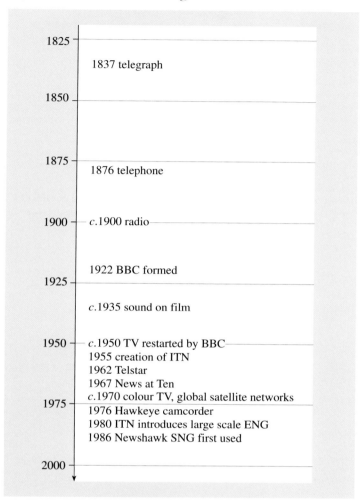

1825

      1837 telegraph

1850

1875

      1876 telephone

1900 — *c.*1900 radio

      1922 BBC formed
1925

      *c.*1935 sound on film

1950 — *c.*1950 TV restarted by BBC
      1955 creation of ITN
      1962 Telstar
      1967 News at Ten
      *c.*1970 colour TV, global satellite networks
1975
      1976 Hawkeye camcorder
      1980 ITN introduces large scale ENG
      1986 Newshawk SNG first used

2000

Figure 28   Time line for the answer to Activity 7

Activity 8

The example which I thought indicated technology push was the use of cinema for newsreels:

> The visual power of cinema as a news medium was quickly recognised and organisations such as British Movietone News and Pathe News soon established themselves with 'newsreels' which were a compilation of the week's best visual stories shot and made on high-quality 35 mm film.
>
> Taylor (1995)

I thought that the clearest example of demand pull was the development of the Newshawk for satellite newsgathering:

> Well, there were still large areas of the world which did not have a wideband cable infrastructure or possess large expensive satellite ground stations and these became the next technological battleground.
>
> These communication dead spots provided the challenge to fire the development of transportable ground stations.
>
> In 1985 ITN formed an alliance with the IBA and McMichael Electronics to develop the world's first SNG uplinks – the Newshawk – which we first used in 1986.
>
> Taylor (1995)

Activity 9

Of Taylor's suggestions for where digital methods promised improvements, the area that I particularly noticed was number 5, multiskilling, because Higgins explicitly discusses this, and gives examples of:

> a cameraman who can record sound and edit tape; a reporter who can also edit tape and/or shoot video and record sound ... or a microwave technician who can operate a camera and edit.
>
> Higgins (2004)

Higgins says that the multiskilling was motivated by the need to reduce costs. Assuming the desired outcomes was realised, this is evidence of number 8, lower operating costs.

Several of the others are implied by Higgins, although maybe not made explicit. For example, he describes the use of laptop computers to do editing in the field. This is likely to deliver 'faster post-production' and 'greater editorial freedom'.

Activity 12

A device, such as a microphone, which converts energy or information from one medium to another is called a transducer.

Activity 14

811 pixels horizontally by 508 pixels vertically gives a total of $811 \times 508 = 411\ 988$ pixels. To two significant figures that is 410 000, or 4.1×10^{5}, using scientific notation.

Activity 17

The distance in metres is given by:

$$d = 0.3\,t = 0.3 \times 14 = 4.2$$

So the distance is 4.2 m.

Activity 19

(a) DVD and some types of flash memory allow random access, but tape does not. Tape is written and read sequentially.

(b) Flash memory is solid state. Tape and DVDs require moving parts to read and write data.

Activity 20

We are told that a PCMCIA card can store five hours at 25 Mbps and that HD TV (high-definition television) runs at 100 Mbps, which is four times the data rate. This indicates that a PCMCIA card should be able to store 5/4 hours, which is 1 hour and 15 minutes, of HD TV.

Activity 21

1 kΩ = 1000 Ω, so the current is given by:

$$i = \frac{v}{r} = \frac{1}{1000}\,\text{A} = 0.001\ \text{A} = 1\,\text{mA}$$

Activity 23

The relationship between capacity, i and t was presented in the course text in two forms:

$$\text{capacity} = i \times t$$

and

$$t = \frac{\text{capacity}}{i}$$

From either of these, and from what you were told previously, you can see that capacity is the quantity that should go at the top of the triangle, so that the triangle is in either of the forms shown in Figure 29.

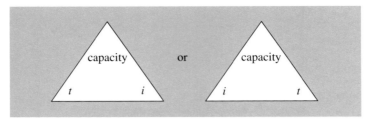

Figure 29   Formula triangle relating battery capacity to current and running time

Activity 24

(a) capacity = $i \times t$ = 0.4 × 10 Ah = 4 Ah

(b) time battery can be used at 0.3 A:

$$t = \frac{\text{capacity}}{i} = \frac{4}{0.3} = 13.33 \text{ hours (to two decimal places)}$$

This is 13 hours and 20 minutes.

Activity 25

1   AA, NiCd. Capacity of 0.8 Ah, so it can run for 0.8/0.1 h = 8 hours.

2   AA NiMH. Capacity of 2.1 Ah, so it can run for 2.1/0.1 h = 21 hours.

3   C NiCd. Capacity of 1.7 Ah, so it can run for 1.7/0.1 h = 17 hours.

4   C NiMH. Capacity of 3.5 Ah, so it can run for 3.5/0.1 h = 35 hours.

Activity 27

To get 3.6 volts from NiCd or NiMH cells, which are each 1.2 volts, three cells would need to be connected in series, as shown in Figure 30.

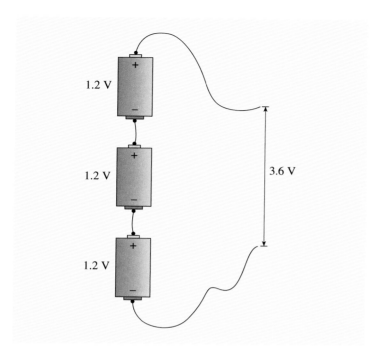

Figure 30 Cells connected in series, for the answer to Activity 26

Activity 30

The pulse travels 200 m in 1 microsecond, so it takes 3 microseconds to travel 600 m. The pulse will be as in Figure 31.

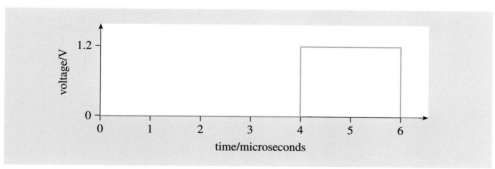

Figure 31 A pulse 600 metres along the wires, for the answer to Activity 30

Activity 32

(a) You need to use the formula triangle from the answer to Activity 23. If you know time and capacity, you can see by covering i (current) that current will be given by:

$$i = \frac{\text{capacity}}{t}$$

(b) If the capacity is 1.8 Ah and the time is 20 hours, the maximum current is:

$$i = \frac{1.8}{20} = 0.09 \text{ A}$$

Activity 34

We need the time, so we use:

$$\text{Propagation time} = \frac{\text{distance}}{\text{speed}}$$

We first write the distance and speed in consistent units. The speed is in metres per second, m/s. The distance is in kilometres, so we need to change it to metres. 1 kilometre is 1000 metres, so 4000 km is $4\,000 \times 10^3$ m $= 4 \times 10^6$ m.

So,

$$\text{Propagation time (delay)} = \frac{4 \times 10^6}{2 \times 10^8} \text{ s} = \frac{4\,000\,000}{200\,000\,000} = 0.02 \text{ s}$$

REFERENCES

Higgins, J. (2004) *Introduction to SNG and ENG Microwave*, Elsevier Focal Press, Oxford.

ITN (2005) *About ITN* Independent Television News Limited [online] http://www.itn.co.uk/index.shtml [Accessed 7 January 2005]

Jones, J. and Seenan, G. (2004) 'The camera today? You can't trust it. Hockney sparks a debate', *The Guardian*, 4 March 2004.

Northedge, A., Thomas, J., Lane, A. and Peasgood, A. (1997) *The Sciences Good Study Guide* , Milton Keynes, The Open University.

Pax, S. (2003) 'I became the profane pervert Arab blogger', *The Guardian*, 9 September 2003.

Taylor, E. V. (1995) 'From newsreels to real news', paper presented at a colloquium entitled *Capturing the Action: Changes in Newsgathering*, Institution of Electrical Engineers, London.

Taylor, E. V. (2004) 'Real news meets IT', [online] T175, http://students.open.ac.uk/technology/courses/t175, The Open University.

ACKNOWLEDGEMENTS

Grateful acknowledgement is made to the following sources for permission to reproduce material within this book.

Text

Taylor E.V., (1995), 'From Newsreels to Real News', *Capturing the Action: Changes in Newsgathering Technology* © 1995 The Institute of Electrical Engineers.

Higgins J., (2004), 'Introduction to SNG and ENG Microwave' Elsevier Science.

Pax S., (2003) 'I Became The Profane Pervert Arab Blogger', The Guardian 9th September 2003. Copyright © 2003 S. Pax. Reproduced with permission.

Figures

Figure 6: www.nanoelectronics.jp

Figure 27: The Cottingley Fairies © Mary Evans Picture Library